Dino Discoveries

Teacher's Guide

Unit 10

Note: See New and Important Objectives on page 2 for a complete list of skills taught and reviewed.

Critical Foundations in Primary Reading

Marilyn Sprick, Ann Watanabe, Karen Akiyama-Paik, and Shelley V. Jones

Sopris West®
EDUCATIONAL SERVICES
A Cambium Learning® Company
BOSTON, MA • LONGMONT, CO

ISBN 13-digit: 978-1-60218-533-3
ISBN 10-digit: 1-60218-533-6

7 8 9 10 11 B&B 16 15 14 13 12

166932/6-12

Table of Contents

Unit 10

Dino Discoveries

How to Teach the Lessons

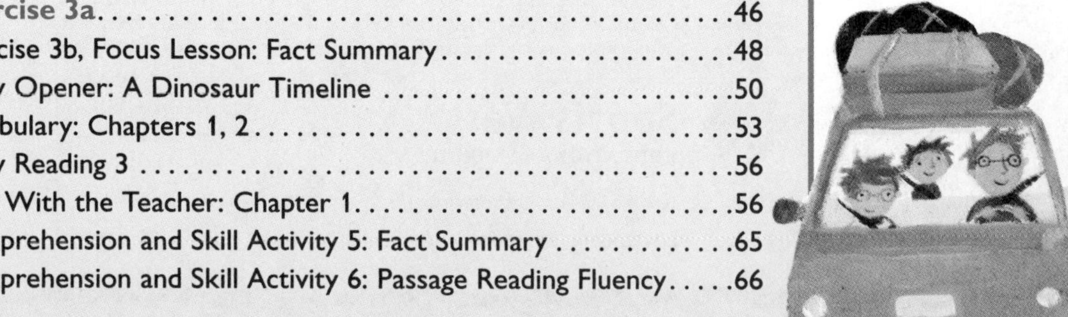

End of the Unit

Read Well 2 Sequence and Sound Pronunciation Guide

Letter Sounds and Combinations

Cumulative Review of *Read Well 1* Sounds and Combinations (Ss, Ee, ee, Mm, Aa, Dd, th, Nn, Tt, Ww, Ii, Th, Hh, Cc, Rr, ea, sh, Sh, Kk, -ck, oo, ar, wh, Wh, ĕ, -y as in fly, Ll, Oo, Bb, all, Gg, Ff, Uu, er, oo as in book, Yy, a schwa, Pp, ay, Vv, Qq, Jj, Xx, or, Zz, a_e, -y as in baby, i_e, ou, ow as in cow, ch, Ch, ai, igh, o_e, ir) and:

Unit 2	Unit 3			Unit 5	Unit 6
aw	ew	ue	u_e	ow	ge
/aw/	/o͞o/	/o͞o/	/o͞o/	/ōōō/	/j/
Paw	**Crew**	**Blue**	**Flute**	**Snow**	**Page**
Voiced	Voiced	Voiced	Bossy E Voiced	Voiced (Long)	Voiced
Unit 6	**Unit 7**		**Unit 8**		**Unit 10**
-dge	ci	ce	kn	ph	oa
/j/	/sss/	/sss/	/nnn/	/fff/	/ōōō/
Badge	**Circle**	**Center**	**Knee**	**Phone**	**Boat**
Voiced	Unvoiced	Unvoiced	Voiced	Unvoiced	Voiced (Long)
Unit 11		**Unit 12**		**Unit 13**	
oi	ea	gi	au	oy	
/oi/	/ĕĕĕ/	/j/	/au/	/oy/	
Point	**Bread**	**Giraffe**	**Astronaut**	**Boy**	
Voiced	Voiced (Short)	Voiced	Voiced	Voiced	

Affixes (including morphographs—affixes taught with meaning) and Open Syllables

Cumulative Review of *Read Well 1* Affixes (-ed, -en, -es, -ing, -ly, -s, -y, -tion) and:

Unit 2	Unit 3		Unit 5		Unit 6
re-	un-	ex-	o	-ful	bi-
Means again as in reread	**Means not** as in unhappy	as in excited	Open syllable /ō/ as in open and moment	**Means full of** as in colorful	**Means two** as in bicycle
Unit 7	**Unit 8**	**Unit 11**	**Unit 12**	**Unit 13**	
de-	-able	i	be-	-ous	dis-
as in detective	as in comfortable	Open syllable /ī/ as in silence and pilot	as in before	as in enormous	as in discover
Unit 14		**Unit 15**		**Unit 16**	
-al	-ible	-or	-ment	-ic	pre-
as in animal	as in flexible	**Means one who** as in actor	as in apartment	as in scientific	**Means before** as in preview
Unit 17		**Unit 18**		**Unit 19**	
-ity	-sion	-ness	-less	in-	im-
as in activity	as in permission	as in fairness	**Means without** as in helpless	as in insert	**Means not** as in impossible

Introduction
Dino Discoveries

Story Notes

Dinosaurs have fascinated people for generations, inspiring flights of fantasy, exploration, and scientific inquiry.

Going on a Dino Dig: In Unit 2, the Wrights had been asked to join a dino dig. Follow their adventures as they join an expedition. Young Albert goes missing but ends up saving the day.

A Dinosaur Timeline: Students read an expository selection and learn when the dinosaurs lived, where they lived, and how we know about them. With this selection, your students will begin developing a historical perspective of our knowledge of dinosaurs.

There's A Dinosaur in My Bed: This imaginative story will get your students laughing and thinking creatively.

CAUTION
(Reminder)
Do not read the Read Aloud recommendations during small group instruction. Reserve this time for students to read.

Recommended Read Alouds

The *Read Well 2* suggested Read Alouds enhance small group instruction—providing opportunities to further build background knowledge and vocabulary.

Daniel's Dinosaurs: A True Story of Discovery by Charles Helm
Nonfiction
This is the true story of two young boys in British Columbia who find dinosaur tracks near the foothills of the Rocky Mountains. The discovery leads paleontologists to the site of 93-million-year-old dinosaur bones.

***Read Well* Connections**
This true story complements the fictional account of a fossil hunt in "Going on a Dino Dig." It also provides further insights into how scientists learn more about these extinct creatures.

NOTE FROM THE AUTHORS

TEACH WITH ENTHUSIASM

Students are motivated by your enthusiasm.

- As you read, make connections: I've always wondered what people long ago must have thought about dinosaur bones. I wonder if that's where they got the idea of giants and dragons. What do you think?
- Model your response as a reader: I like Albert. He reminds me of . . .
- Think aloud and demonstrate expressive reading: Listen to that sentence again. "They destroyed many bones by using dynamite to blast away rock." How silly! Marsh and Cope destroyed bones that were millions and millions of years old. Why do you think they did that?

New and Important Objectives

A Research-Based Reading Program

Phonemic Awareness
Phonics
Fluency
Vocabulary
Comprehension

Phonological and Phonemic Awareness

Segmenting; Blending; Rhyming; Onset and Rime;
Counting Syllables

Phonics

Cumulative Letter Sounds and Combinations

Review • Ss, Ee, ee, Mm, Aa, Dd, th, Nn, Tt, Ww, Ii, Th, Hh, Cc, Rr, ea, sh, Sh, Kk, -ck, oo, ar, wh, Wh, ĕ, -y (as in fly), Ll, Oo, Bb, all, Gg, Ff, Uu, er, oo (as in book), Yy, a (schwa), Pp, ay, Vv, Qq, Jj, Xx, or, Zz, a_e, -y (as in baby), i_e, ou, ow (as in cow), ch, Ch, ai, igh, o_e, ir, aw, ew, ue, u_e, ow (as in snow), ge, -dge, ci, ce, kn, ph

Cumulative Affixes, Morphographs, and Open Syllables

Review • -ed, -en, -er, -es, -est, -ing, -ly, -s, -y, -tion, re-, un-, ex-, o, -ful, bi-, de-, -able

★New Letter Sounds, Combinations, Affixes, and Morphographs

oa (as in boat) • boast, boasted, coach, coast, coat, croak, float, groan, load, moan, roach, road, roam, roamed, soap, toad, toast

★New Proper Nouns

Antarctica, Argentinosaurus, Brachiosaurus, Braille, Charles Marsh, Cretaceous, Edward Cope, Einstein, Hadrosaurus, Knight, Louis, New Jersey, New York, Pangaea, Plateosaurus, Ralph, Sue, Sue's, Tyrannosaurus rex, Wilbur, Wright's

★New Contractions

'em

★New Abbreviations

Dr., SUV

* **Known Pattern Words With Affixes**, **Known Tricky Words With Affixes**, and **Known Multisyllabic Words With Affixes** have base words students have previously read. The words are new in this unit because they have not been previously read with the affix.

★= New in this unit

Phonics (continued)

★New Pattern Words

barely, bore, boring, crates, crouch, crouched, east, fund, funding, lab, laid, leaned, leg, pant, pup, sip, sipping, slices, spied, steal, tip, tipped, whoop, whooped, woke, wrong

*__Known Pattern Words With Affixes__ • biweekly, brushes, calling, chipped, clears, freely, games, guesses, hooted, largest, nearly, notes, picks, prints, rebuild, remade, roots, rushing, shipped, shows, taller, towns, tracks, unlike, woods

★New Compound and Hyphenated Words

campsite, footprints, half-dozen, highway, paintbrushes, peanut, riverbank, saber-toothed, thighbone, timeline, yee-haw

★Other New Multisyllabic Words

apart, appear, bicker, bickered, carnivores, chisels, coffee, complete, continued, cozy, creatures, definitely, directions, dragon, dynamite, expedition, explore, exploring, extinct, hammer, hammers, hollering, hunter, hunters, include, including, lizard, locate, number, obsessed, ornithopods, plaster, possible, rather, realize, realized, remains, rescue, sandwich, scramble, scrambled, skeleton, skeletons, theropods, tidy, topic, traffic, twinkle, twinkled, velociraptor, weary

*__Known Multisyllabic Words With Affixes__ • continents, fascinating, fossils, hesitating, organized, rumbled

★New Tricky Words

break, died, either, enormous, field, museum, period, research, shovels, terrible, tiger, wars

*__Known Tricky Words With Affixes__ • brother's, discovering, fours, oceans, talking, mountains, uncovered, untouched, weighed

Fluency

Accuracy, Expression, Phrasing, Rate

Vocabulary

New • bicker, boast, crouch, definitely, determined, dinosaur, expedition, extinct, fascinate, fossil, insist, locate, obsessed, organize, realize, remains, roam, weary

Review • adventure, amazed, bittersweet, curious, destroy, fossil, hesitate, imagine, ordinary, protect, vast

Reviewed in Context • adventure, amazed, amazing, belongings, bittersweet, continent, curious, destroy, disappointed, fascinated, herbivore, hesitate, imagine, neighborhood, ordinary, perfect, plain, vast

Idioms and Expressions

New • save the day

Comprehension

Unit Genres

Fiction • Realistic Narrative

Nonfiction • Expository

Fiction • Imaginative

Comprehension Processes

Build Knowledge: Factual, Procedural, Conceptual

Day	1	2	3	4	5	6
Remember						
Defining						
Identifying (recalling)	S,C	S,C	E,S,C	S,C	E,S,C	C
Using	S				S	
Understand						
Defining (in your own words)	S,C		S		S	
Describing		S		S		
Explaining (rephrasing)	S	C	S	S	S,C	S
Illustrating	C	C			C	
Sequencing		C		C		
Summarizing		S	S,C	S	S	
Using	S	S	S	S	S	C
Visualizing	C	C	S			
Apply						
Demonstrating		S				
Explaining (unstated)	S		S		S	C
Illustrating	C	C				
Inferring	S,C	S	S	S	S	S,C
Making Connections (relating)	S,C			S		
Predicting	S	S	S		S	
Using	S,C	S	S	S	S	S
Analyze						
Classifying						
Comparing/Contrasting				C		
Distinguishing Cause/Effect						
Drawing Conclusions			S			
Inferring	S			S	S	S
Evaluate						
Making Judgments					S	
Responding (personal)	S,C			S	S	C
Create						
Generating Ideas			E,S	S	E,S,C	C

E = Exercise, S = Storybook, C = Comprehension & Skill

Comprehension *(continued)*

Skills and Strategies

Day	1	2	3	4	5	6
Priming Background Knowledge	S		S			
Setting a Purpose for Reading	S			S		
Answering Questions	S	S,C	S	S	S,C	S
Asking Questions			S	S	S	
Visualizing	C	C	S			
Comprehension Monitoring/Fix Ups						
Does it Make Sense?	C	C	E,C		E,C	
Looking Back		S			C	
Restating						
Summarizing						
Main Idea						
Retelling						
Supporting Details						
Understanding Text Structure						
Title, Author, Illustrator	S	S	S	S	S	
Fact or Fiction						
Genre (Classifying)	S		S	E		
Narrative						
Setting						
Main Character/Traits (Characterization)	S	S				
Goal					S	
Problem/Solution	S	S,C				
Action/Events/Sequence	S,C	S			E	
Outcome/Conclusion		C			E	
Lesson/Author's Message						
Expository						
Subject/Topic		C	E,S,C	S,C	S	C
Heading			S	S,C		
Supporting Details (Facts/Information)		S,C	E,S,C	S	S	
Main Idea		C				C
Using Graphic Organizers						
Chart						
Diagram (labeling)						
Hierarchy (topic/detail)		C				
K-W-L			S		S	
Map (locating, labeling)						
Matrix (compare/contrast)				C		
Sequence (linear, cycle, cause and effect)		C		C		
Story Map						
Web						

E = Exercise, S = Storybook, C = Comprehension & Skill

Comprehension *(continued)*

Study Skills

Day	1	2	3	4	5	6
Alphabetical Order	C					
Following Directions						
Locating Information			S,C	S		
Note Taking						
Previewing						
Reviewing		S	S		S	
Test Taking		C		C		C
Using Glossary		S	S		S	
Using Table of Contents	S		S			
Viewing	S	S	S	S	S	
Verifying					S	

Writing in Response to Reading

Day	1	2	3	4	5	6
Sentence Completion	C	C			C	C
Making Lists			C			C
Sentence Writing	C	C				C
Story Retell/Summary						
Fact Summary			C			
Paragraph Writing			C	C	C	
Report Writing						
Open-Ended Response						
Creative Writing					C	

Writing Traits

(Addressed within the context of Writing in Response to Reading)

Day	1	2	3	4	5	6
Ideas and Content						
Elaborating/Generating			C		C	C
Organization						
Introduction					E,C	
Topic Sentence			C	C		
Supporting Details						
Sequencing						
Word Choice						
Sophisticated Words (Tier 2 and 3)	C		C		E,C	C
Conventions						
Capital	C	C	C		C	C
Ending Punctuation	C	C	C	C	C	C
Other (commas, quotation marks)	C					
Presentation						
Handwriting			C	C	C	C
Neatness			C	C	C	C

E = Exercise, S = Storybook, C = Comprehension & Skill

Daily Lesson Planning

LESSON PLAN FORMAT

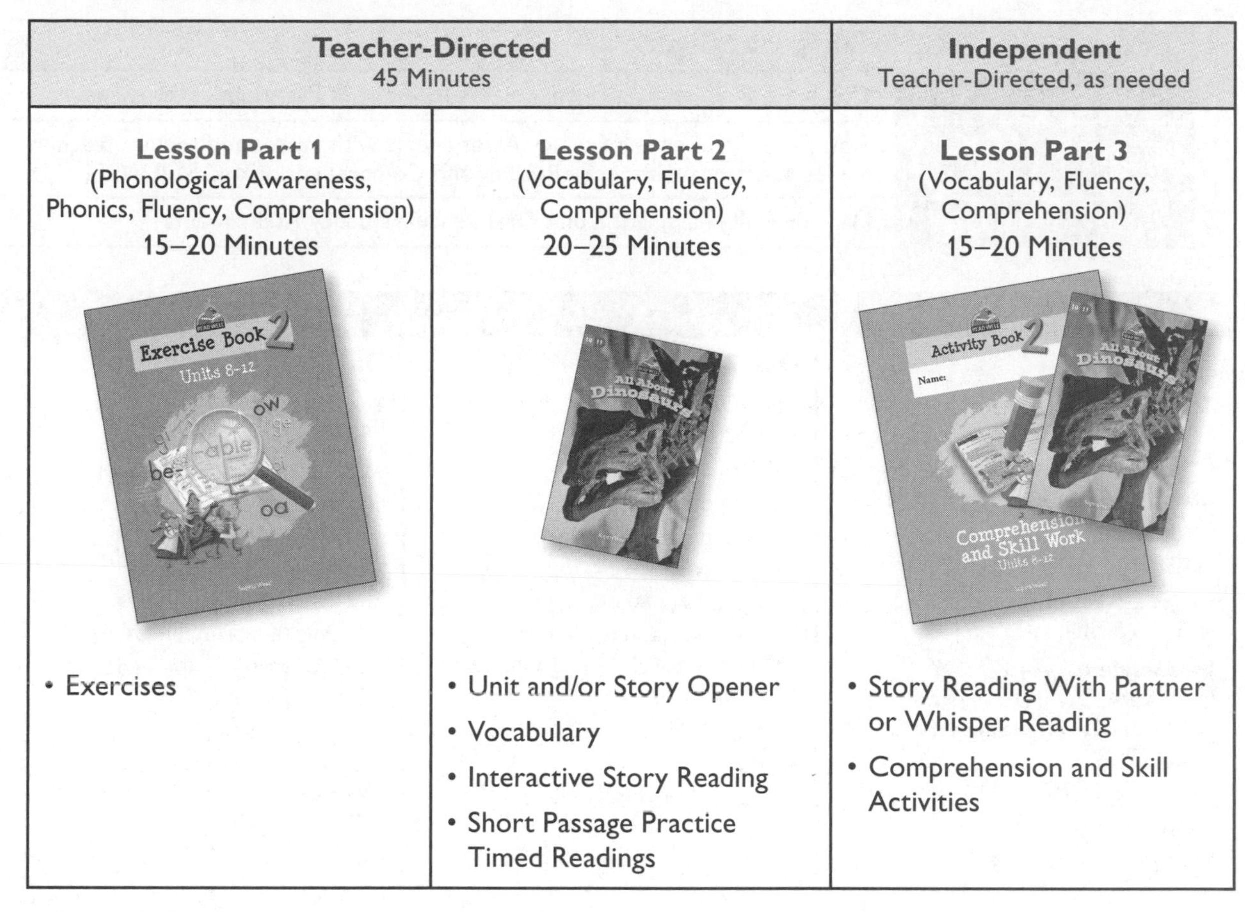

Teacher-Directed 45 Minutes		Independent Teacher-Directed, as needed
Lesson Part 1 (Phonological Awareness, Phonics, Fluency, Comprehension) 15–20 Minutes	**Lesson Part 2** (Vocabulary, Fluency, Comprehension) 20–25 Minutes	**Lesson Part 3** (Vocabulary, Fluency, Comprehension) 15–20 Minutes
• Exercises	• Unit and/or Story Opener • Vocabulary • Interactive Story Reading • Short Passage Practice Timed Readings	• Story Reading With Partner or Whisper Reading • Comprehension and Skill Activities

HOMEWORK

Read Well 2 Homework (blackline masters of new *Read Well 2* passages) provides an opportunity for children to celebrate accomplishments with parents. Homework should be sent home on routine days.

ORAL READING FLUENCY ASSESSMENT

Upon completion of this unit, assess each student and proceed to Unit 11, as appropriate.

WRITTEN ASSESSMENT

Upon completion of this unit, students will be administered a Written Assessment that can be found on page 67 in the students' *Activity Book 2*.

Note: See Making Decisions for additional assessment information.

DIFFERENTIATED LESSON PLANS

The differentiated lesson plans illustrate how materials can be used for students with various learning needs. As you set up your unit plan, always include *Read Well 2* Exercises and Story Reading on a daily basis. Unit 10 includes 6-, 8-, 9-, 10-, and 11-Day Plans.

Plans	For groups that:
6-DAY	Complete Oral Reading Fluency Assessments with Passes and Strong Passes
8-DAY	Complete Oral Reading Fluency Assessments with Passes and require teacher-guided assistance with Story Reading and Comprehension and Skill Work
9-, 10-, or 11-DAY	Have difficulty passing the unit Oral Reading Fluency Assessments

<table>
<tr><th colspan="3">6-DAY PLAN</th></tr>
<tr>
<td>Day 1
Teacher-Directed
• Exercise 1
• Unit and Story Opener: Dino Discoveries, Going on a Dino Dig
• Vocabulary, Ch. 1, 2
• Going on a Dino Dig, Ch. 1
• Guide practice, as needed, on Comp & Skill 1, 2
Independent Work
• On Your Own: Partner or Whisper Read, Going on a Dino Dig, Ch. 2
• Comp & Skill 1, 2
Homework
• Homework Passage 1</td>
<td>Day 2
Teacher-Directed
• Exercise 2
• Vocabulary, Ch. 3
• Going on a Dino Dig, Ch. 3
• Guide practice, as needed, on Comp & Skill 3, 4
Independent Work
• Repeated Reading: Partner or Whisper Read, Going on a Dino Dig, Ch. 3
• Comp & Skill 3, 4
Homework
• Homework Passage 2</td>
<td>Day 3
Teacher-Directed
• Exercise 3a
• Exercise 3b: Focus Lesson
• Story Opener: A Dinosaur Timeline
• K-W-L (modified)
• Vocabulary, Ch. 1, 2
• A Dinosaur Timeline, Ch. 1
• Guide practice, as needed, on Comp & Skill 5, 6
Independent Work
• Repeated Reading: Partner or Whisper Read, A Dinosaur Timeline, Ch. 1
• Comp & Skill 5, 6
Homework
• Homework Passage 3</td>
</tr>
<tr>
<td>Day 4
Teacher-Directed
• Exercise 4
• A Dinosaur Timeline, Ch. 2
• Guide practice, as needed, on Comp & Skill 7, 8
Independent Work
• Repeated Reading: Partner or Whisper Read, A Dinosaur Timeline, Ch. 2
• Comp & Skill 7, 8
Homework
• Homework Passage 4</td>
<td>Day 5
Teacher-Directed
• Exercise 5a
• Exercise 5b: Focus Lesson
• Vocabulary, Ch. 3
• A Dinosaur Timeline, Ch. 3
• K-W-L (modified)
• Guide practice, as needed, on Comp & Skill 9, 10
Independent Work
• Repeated Reading: Partner or Whisper Read, A Dinosaur Timeline, Ch. 3
• Comp & Skill 9, 10
Homework
• Homework Passage 5</td>
<td>Day 6
Teacher-Directed
• Exercise 6
• Fluency, There's a Dinosaur in My Bed
Independent Work
• Repeated Reading: Partner or Whisper Read, There's a Dinosaur in My Bed
• Written Assessment
• Oral Reading Fluency Assessment*
Homework
• Homework Passage 6</td>
</tr>
</table>

* The Oral Reading Fluency Assessments are individually administered by the teacher while students are working on their Written Assessments.

8-DAY PLAN • *Pre-Intervention*

Day 1	Day 2	Day 3	Day 4
Teacher-Directed • Exercise 1 • Unit and Story Opener: Dino Discoveries, Going on a Dino Dig • Vocabulary, Ch. 1, 2 • Going on a Dino Dig, Ch. 1 • Guide practice, as needed, on Comp & Skill 1 **Independent Work** • Repeated Reading: Partner or Whisper Read, Going on a Dino Dig, Ch. 1 • Comp & Skill 1 **Homework** • Homework Passage 1	**Teacher-Directed** • Review Exercise 1 • Going on a Dino Dig, Ch. 2 • Guide practice, as needed, on Comp & Skill 2 **Independent Work** • Repeated Reading: Partner or Whisper Read, Going on a Dino Dig, Ch. 2 • Comp & Skill 2 **Homework** • Comp & Skill 2 (Passage Fluency)	**Teacher-Directed** • Exercise 2 • Vocabulary, Ch. 3 • Going on a Dino Dig, Ch. 3 • Guide practice, as needed, on Comp & Skill 3, 4 **Independent Work** • Repeated Reading: Partner or Whisper Read, Going on a Dino Dig, Ch. 3 • Comp & Skill 3, 4 **Homework** • Homework Passage 2	**Teacher-Directed** • Exercise 3a • Exercise 3b: Focus Lesson • Story Opener: A Dinosaur Timeline • K-W-L (modified) • Vocabulary, Ch. 1, 2 • A Dinosaur Timeline, Ch. 1 • Guide practice, as needed, on Comp & Skill 5, 6 **Independent Work** • Repeated Reading: Partner or Whisper Read, A Dinosaur Timeline, Ch. 1 • Comp & Skill 5, 6 **Homework** • Homework Passage 3
Day 5	**Day 6**	**Day 7**	**Day 8**
Teacher-Directed • Exercise 4 • A Dinosaur Timeline, Ch. 2 • Guide practice, as needed, on Comp & Skill **Independent Work** • Repeated Reading: Partner or Whisper Read, A Dinosaur Timeline, Ch. 2 • Comp & Skill 7, 8 **Homework** • Homework Passage 4	**Teacher-Directed** • Exercise 5a • Vocabulary, Ch. 3 • A Dinosaur Timeline, Ch. 3 • K-W-L (modified) • Guide practice, as needed, on Comp & Skill 9 **Independent Work** • Repeated Reading: Partner or Whisper Read, A Dinosaur Timeline, Ch. 3 • Comp & Skill 9 **Homework** • Homework Passage 4	**Teacher-Directed** • Exercise 5b: Focus Lesson • Review Vocabulary, Ch. 1–3 • Reread A Dinosaur Timeline, Ch. 3 • Guide practice, as needed, on Comp & Skill 10 **Independent Work** • Repeated Reading: Partner or Whisper Read, A Dinosaur Timeline, Ch. 3 • Comp & Skill 10 **Homework** • Comp & Skill 9 (Passage Reading)	**Teacher-Directed** • Exercise 6 • Fluency, There's a Dinosaur in My Bed **Independent Work** • Repeated Reading: Partner or Whisper Read, There's a Dinosaur in My Bed • Written Assessment • Oral Reading Fluency Assessment* **Homework** • Homework Passage 6

9-, 10-, or 11-DAY PLAN • *Intervention*

For Days 1–8, follow 8-Day plan. Add Days 9, 10, 11 as follows:

Day 9 Extra Practice 1	Day 10 Extra Practice 2	Day 11 Extra Practice 3
Teacher-Directed • Decoding Practice • Fluency Passage **Independent Work** • Activity and Word Fluency A **Homework** • Fluency Passage	**Teacher-Directed** • Decoding Practice • Fluency Passage **Independent Work** • Activity and Word Fluency B **Homework** • Fluency Passage	**Teacher-Directed** • Decoding Practice • Fluency Passage **Independent Work** • Activity and Word Fluency A or B • Oral Reading Fluency Assessment* **Homework** • Fluency Passage

Materials and Materials Preparation

Core Lessons

Teacher Materials

***READ WELL 2* MATERIALS**

- Unit 10 Teacher's Guide
- Sound Cards
- Unit 10 Oral Reading Fluency Assessment found on page 108
- Group Assessment Record found in the *Assessment Manual*

SCHOOL SUPPLIES

Stopwatch or watch with a second hand

Student Materials

***READ WELL 2* MATERIALS (for each student)**

- *All About Dinosaurs* storybook
- *Exercise Book 2*
- *Activity Book 2* or copies of Unit 10 Comprehension and Skill Work
- Unit 10 Written Assessment found in *Activity Book 2*, page 67, and on the blackline master CD
- Unit 10 Certificate of Achievement (blackline master, page 109)
- Unit 10 Homework (blackline masters)
  See *Getting Started* for suggested homework routines.

SCHOOL SUPPLIES

Pencils, colors (optional—markers, crayons, or colored pencils)

Make one copy per student of each blackline master, as appropriate for the group.

Note: For new or difficult Comprehension and Skill Activities, make overhead transparencies from the blackline masters. Use the transparencies to demonstrate and guide practice.

FOCUS LESSONS

For Exercises 3b and 5b (Focus Lessons), make overhead transparencies from the blackline masters, write on transparencies placed over the pages, or use paper copies to demonstrate how to complete the lessons.

Extra Practice Lessons

CAUTION

Use these lessons only if needed. Students who need Extra Practice may benefit from one, two, or three lessons.

Student Materials

***READ WELL 2* MATERIALS (for each student, as needed)**

See Extra Practice blackline masters located on the CD.

- Unit 10 Extra Practice 1: Decoding Practice, Fluency Passage, Word Fluency A, and Activity
- Unit 10 Extra Practice 2: Decoding Practice, Fluency Passage, Word Fluency B, and Activity
- Unit 10 Extra Practice 3: Decoding Practice, Fluency Passage, Word Fluency A or B, and Activity

SCHOOL SUPPLIES

Pencils, colors (markers, crayons, or colored pencils), highlighters

Important Tips

Building Oral Reading Fluency
Booster Sessions

Building Oral Reading Fluency

FLUENCY

Fluent reading is characteristic of a reader who is free of the word-identification problems that often hinder comprehension. Fluency is "the ability to read a text quickly, accurately, and with proper expression" (National Reading Panel, 2000, p. 3-1).

ACCURACY

Basic story reading procedures are critical for initially building the accuracy that is required for fluency. On a daily basis, continue to:

- have students track words with their fingers.
- gently correct errors and have students reread.
- record errors and have students practice difficult words between readings.
- repeat the reading for accuracy, as needed.

In *Read Well*, the goal is to read a decodable passage until students read at an "independent reading level" of 98% to 99% accuracy. Accuracy is the gateway to reading text quickly.

QUICKLY AND WITH PROPER EXPRESSION

Read Well fluency practice includes Timed Readings and Repeated Readings. In addition, through modeling and guided practice, Short Passage Practice teaches students to read with expression and to read a little more quickly. Short Passage Practice is included in every odd-numbered lesson.

SHORT PASSAGE PRACTICE

- After students read a passage, demonstrate how to read two or three sentences.
- Model expressive reading at a rate just slightly faster than students read.
- Next, guide expressive and accurate reading. Read with students, using your voice to lead them.
- Then have individual students read the same few sentences, while others finger track and whisper read. Acknowledge students' efforts.

Booster Sessions

Some students require additional practice to meet the desired fluency rates on assessments. For these students, work on fluency in short extra practice sessions. Five extra minutes two or three times a week with a trained instructional assistant, parent volunteer, or older student can ensure a student's success in a challenging group.

FLUENCY PROCEDURES

Once the student is able to read with accuracy, work on fluency. Provide additional practice with *Read Well 2* passages or *Read Well 2* Extra Practice Passages. The following procedures are effective in helping students read quickly and with proper expression:

- Have students do Short Passage Practice. Demonstrate and guide. (See page 86.)
- Time and chart words correct per minute.
- Have students tape record themselves, listen, and mark their own errors. Then rerecord if they wish.
- Ask parents if they can have their child read homework passages two times.
- Use the goal-setting forms at the end of each unit to help students identify what they can do to achieve their personal bests.

  Say something like:
  [Aaron], you are reading really well now. You always read with 99% accuracy and sometimes even 100%. I'd like to help you meet your goal of 110 words correct per minute. I know you can do it. For the next week, Mrs. Schmale said you could stay for a few minutes and really polish up a page. I'm going to have you whisper read, then you and I are going to do a Short Practice Passage. Finally, you get to tape record yourself reading the passage.

  When the student meets his or her goal, say something like:
  [Aaron], you not only hit 110 words correct per minute, you beat your goal. You read 112 words correct per minute! Would you like to pick your favorite passage and read it to the principal? I think she would be delighted to hear you.

How to Teach the Lessons

Teach from this section. Each instructional component is outlined in an easy-to-teach format.

Exercise 1

- Unit and Story Opener: Dino Discoveries, Going on a Dino Dig
- Vocabulary
- Story Reading 1
  With the Teacher: Chapter 1
  On Your Own: Chapter 2
- Comprehension and Skill Activities 1, 2

Exercise 2

- Vocabulary
- Story Reading 2
  With the Teacher: Chapter 3
- Comprehension and Skill Activities 3, 4

Exercise 3a

- Exercise 3b: Focus Lesson
- Story Opener: A Dinosaur Timeline
- Vocabulary
- Story Reading 3
  With the Teacher: Chapter 1
- Comprehension and Skill Activities 5, 6

Exercise 4

- Story Reading 4
  With the Teacher: Chapter 2
- Comprehension and Skill Activities 7, 8

Exercise 5a

- Exercise 5b: Focus Lesson
- Vocabulary
- Story Reading 5
  With the Teacher: Chapter 3
- Comprehension and Skill Activities 9, 10

Exercise 6

- Story Reading 6
  With the Teacher: There's a Dinosaur in My Bed (Fluency)
- Written Assessment

Note: Lessons include daily homework.

❶ SOUND REVIEW

Use selected Sound Cards from Units 1–9.

PACING

Exercise 1 should take about 15 minutes.

★❷ NEW SOUND INTRODUCTION

- Have students look at the picture. Say something like:
  Look at the picture. Say "o-a says /ōōō/ as in boat." (o-a says /ōōō/ as in boat)
  Listen to the o-a words in the sentence. "Look at the toad sitting in the boat."
  Read the sentence. (Look at the toad sitting in the boat.)
  What two words have the /ōōō/ sound? (toad, boat)
- For Row B, have students read the underlined sound, then the word.
- After reading the row, have students go back and read the whole words. Provide repeated practice. Mix group and individual turns.

❸ ACCURACY AND FLUENCY BUILDING

- For each task, have students say any underlined part, then read the word.
- Set a pace. Then have students read the whole words in each task and column.
- Provide repeated practice, building accuracy first, then fluency.

E1. Tricky Words

- For each Tricky Word, have students use the sounds and word parts they know to silently sound out the word. Use the word in a sentence to help with pronunciation.
- If the word is unfamiliar, tell students the word.

dozen	Angel wanted 12 donuts. She wanted one . . . *dozen.*
mountain	There is snow on top of the . . . *mountain.*
talking	If you don't have anything to say, then you shouldn't be . . . *talking.*
pull	When you play tug of war, you . . . *pull* . . . on the rope.
stomach	Another word for your belly is . . . *stomach.*
worry	Don't be upset. Don't . . . *worry.*
worried	When Jake didn't come home on time, his parents . . . *worried.*

- Have students go back and read the whole words in the column.

❹ MULTISYLLABIC WORDS

For each word, have students read the syllables, then the whole word. Use the word in a sentence, as appropriate.

chisels	The cabinetmaker had some tools called . . . *chisels.*
definitely	I'm going for sure. I'm . . . *definitely* . . . going.
organized	She cleaned up her room and got everything . . . *organized.*
traffic	The highway was really busy. There was lots of . . . *traffic.*
directions	We were lost, so Dad stopped to ask for . . . *directions.*
hollering	When she fell, she started . . . *hollering.*

★❺ DINOSAUR WORDS

- Tell students they will be reading dinosaur names or words related to dinosaurs.
- Have students read each word, using the pronunciation guide for help. Demonstrate, as needed.
- Use the word in a sentence, as needed.

★= New in this unit

❻ GENERALIZATION: READING NEW WORDS IN PARAGRAPHS

- Have students read the paragraph silently, then out loud. Tell students to use the sounds and word parts they know to read any difficult words.
- Repeat practice, as needed.

TEAM EXPECTATIONS (Reminder)

Provide a quick review of expectations before starting the lesson.

1. Sit up.
2. Follow directions.
3. Help each other.
4. Work hard and have fun.

Going on a Dino Dig

Unit 10 Exercise 1

Use before Chapters 1 and 2

1. SOUND REVIEW Use selected Sound Cards from Units 1–9.

★2. NEW SOUND INTRODUCTION Introduce the new sound /ōōō/ as in boat.

A oa	boat	Look at the toad sitting in the boat.

B				
load	road	coat	soap	toast

3. ACCURACY AND FLUENCY BUILDING For each column, have students say any underlined part, then read each word. Next, have students read the whole column.

A1 Mixed Practice	B1 Bossy E	C1 Word Endings	D1 Word Endings	E1 Tricky Words
Ralph	slices	tipped	whooped	dozen
rescue	crates	sipping	hooted	mountain
weary	locate	rushing	rumbled	talking
Knight	barely	funding	scrambled	pull
coffee	**B2 Compound Words**	brushes	hammers	stomach
dawn	campsite	**C2 Names**	hesitate	worry
east	footprints	Einstein	hesitating	worried
leaned	highway	Braille	determine	
greet		Louis	determined	
Wilbur				

BUILD ACCURACY AND FLUENCY (Reminder)

For all rows and columns, follow the specific directions, then build accuracy and fluency with whole words.

4. MULTISYLLABIC WORDS Have students read each word part, then read each whole word.

A	chis•els	chisels	def•i•nite•ly	definitely
B	or•ga•nized	organized	traf•fic	traffic
C	dir•ec•tions	directions	hol•ler•ing	hollering

★5. DINOSAUR WORDS Have students use the sounds and word parts they know and the pronunciation guide to read the word.

Velociraptor	Vuh-law-si-rap-ter

GENERALIZATION (Reminder)

The generalization task provides an opportunity for you to informally assess students' ability to read new words that have not been pretaught.

6. GENERALIZATION Have students read the paragraph silently, then out loud. (New words: Dr., expedition, terrible)

Dr. Knight wandered into the woods, singing a happy tune. He was excited about leaving soon on an expedition to find dinosaur bones. His son Albert hoped they would find the most frightening and terrible dinosaur ever found. "Yes," thought Dr. Knight, "if we find a new dinosaur, we will be famous."

17

COMPREHENSION PROCESSES

Remember, Understand, Apply

PROCEDURES

1. Introducing the Storybook and Theme

Identifying—Title; Inferring; Viewing

Tell students the title of their new storybook and discuss the theme. Say something like:

Everyone, look at the cover of your new storybook.

What's the title of your new storybook? (All About Dinosaurs)

What do you think this story is about? (dinosaurs)

That's right. Look at the picture. What do you see?

2. Introducing the Unit and Story

Using the Table of Contents; Identifying—Titles, Genre; Predicting

Tell students the title of their new unit and story. Say something like:

We're starting a new book. Turn to the Table of Contents.

The title of Unit 10 is "Dino Discoveries." Touch the unit title. What's the title of this unit? (Dino Discoveries)

What do you think this unit will be about? (discovering dinosaurs, finding dinosaurs)

What's the first story called? (Going on a Dino Dig)

That's right. "Going on a Dino Dig" is about the Wright family—Ben; his dad; and his brother, Albert.

What do you think is going to happen in this story? Do you think the story is fact or fiction? Why?

Look at page 3. What's the name of the second story? (A Dinosaur Timeline)

"A Dinosaur Timeline" should be fun. This selection is factual, so what do we call it? (nonfiction)

Now find the title page for "Going on a Dino Dig." What page should we turn to? (page 7)

Note: If your group read Unit 2, you may wish to briefly review what students remember about the Wrights.

TABLE OF CONTENTS

UNIT 10 • Dino Discoveries

UNIT 10
Dino Discoveries

6

Going on a Dino Dig

by Marilyn Sprick
illustrated by Jana Christy

Look at the picture. The Wrights are packing up. How do you think the family feels?[1]

7

3. Introducing the Title Page

Have students look at the picture on page 7. Ask questions as indicated by the gray text.

Everyone, turn to page 7, the title page of "Going on a Dino Dig." Look at the picture . . . Nod your head if you would like to go on a dino dig.

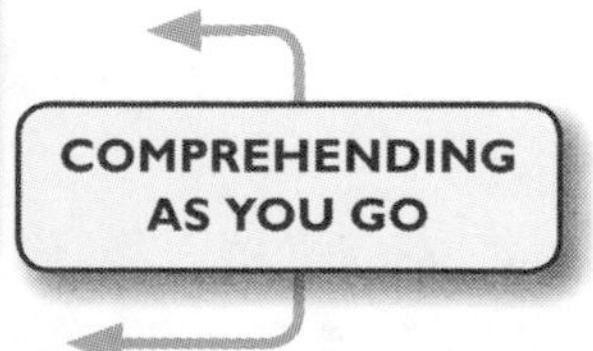

❶ **Understand:** Viewing, Inferring (The family is excited, happy . . .)

COMPREHENSION PROCESSES

Understand, Apply

PROCEDURES

Introducing Vocabulary

★definitely ★expedition
★weary ★locate
★organize ★determined

- For each vocabulary word, have students read the word by parts, then read the whole word.
- Read the student-friendly explanations to students as they follow with their fingers. Then have students use the vocabulary word by following the gray text.
- Review and discuss the photos and illustrations.

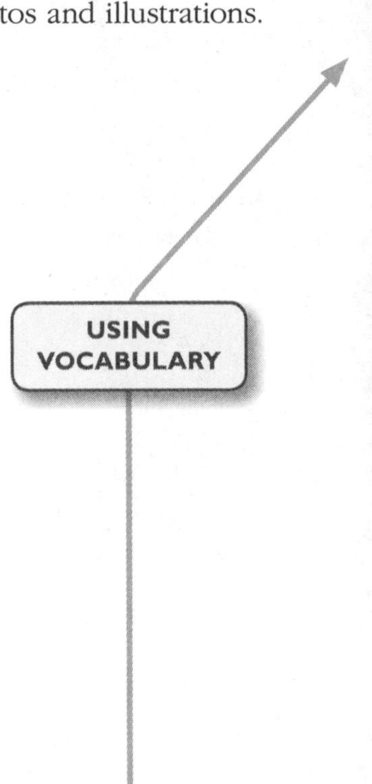

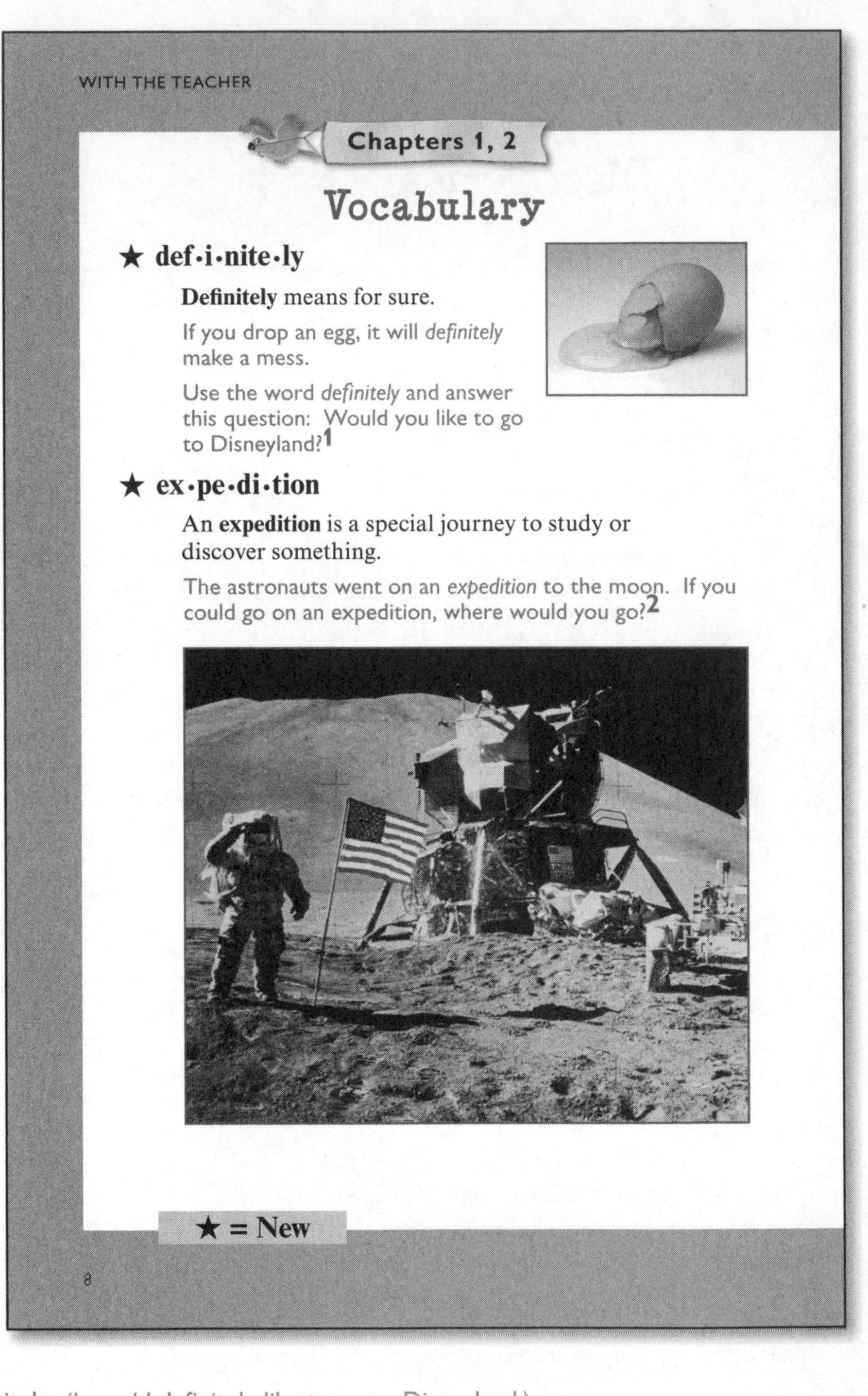

WITH THE TEACHER

Chapters 1, 2

Vocabulary

★ **def·i·nite·ly**

Definitely means for sure.

If you drop an egg, it will *definitely* make a mess.

Use the word *definitely* and answer this question: Would you like to go to Disneyland?[1]

★ **ex·pe·di·tion**

An **expedition** is a special journey to study or discover something.

The astronauts went on an *expedition* to the moon. If you could go on an expedition, where would you go?[2]

★ = New

8

❶ **Understand:** Using Vocabulary—definitely (I would definitely like to go to Disneyland.)

❷ **Apply:** Making Connections; Using Vocabulary—expedition (If I could go on an expedition, I would go to Africa to see the wildlife. I would go on a dino dig. I would . . .)

★= New in this unit

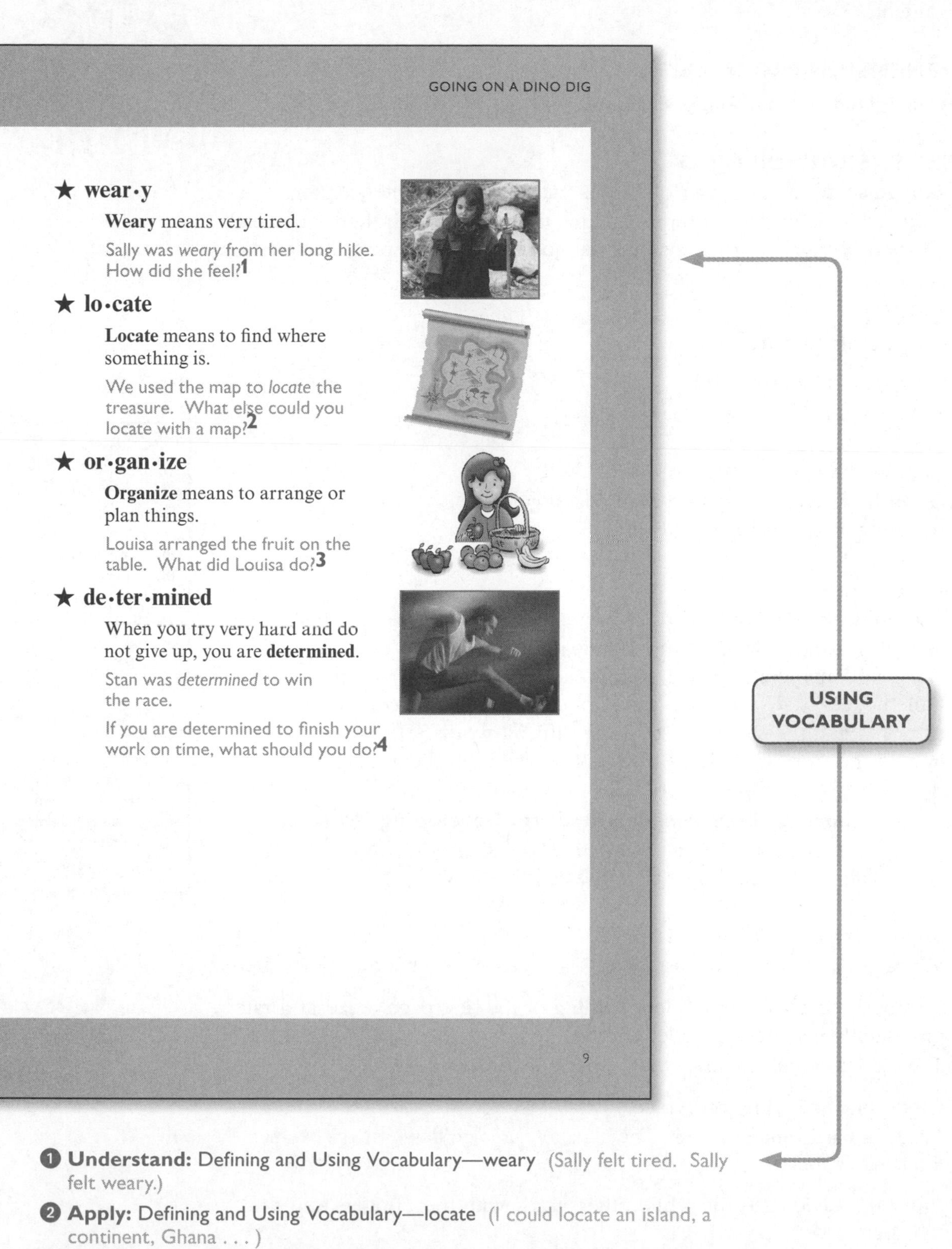
GOING ON A DINO DIG

★ **wear·y**

Weary means very tired.

Sally was *weary* from her long hike. How did she feel?1

★ **lo·cate**

Locate means to find where something is.

We used the map to *locate* the treasure. What else could you locate with a map?2

★ **or·gan·ize**

Organize means to arrange or plan things.

Louisa arranged the fruit on the table. What did Louisa do?3

★ **de·ter·mined**

When you try very hard and do not give up, you are **determined**.

Stan was *determined* to win the race.

If you are determined to finish your work on time, what should you do?4

9

❶ **Understand:** Defining and Using Vocabulary—weary (Sally felt tired. Sally felt weary.)

❷ **Apply:** Defining and Using Vocabulary—locate (I could locate an island, a continent, Ghana . . .)

❸ **Understand:** Defining and Using Vocabulary—organize (She organized the fruit.)

❹ **Understand:** Defining Vocabulary—determined (I should keep working hard until I am done.)

CHAPTER 1 INSTRUCTIONS

Students read Chapter 1 with the teacher and Chapter 2 on their own.
Note: If you're working on an 8- to 11-Day Plan, you will read Chapter 2 with students.

COMPREHENSION PROCESSES

Remember, Understand, Apply, Evaluate

COMPREHENSION BUILDING

- Encourage students to answer questions with complete sentences.
- If students have difficulty comprehending, think aloud with them or reread the portion of the story that answers the question. Then repeat the question.

PROCEDURES

1. Introducing Chapter 1

Identifying—Title; Inferring

Discuss the title and main characters.
Say something like:
What's the title of this chapter? (The E-Mail)
Look at the picture. Where are the Wrights going?
(They are going on a long trip.)

2. First Reading

- Ask questions and discuss the story as indicated by the gray text.
- Mix group and individual turns, independent of your voice.
  Have students work toward a group accuracy goal of 0–5 errors.
  Quietly keep track of errors made by all students in the group.
- After reading the story, practice any difficult words.
  Reread the story if students have not reached the accuracy goal.

3. Second Reading, Short Passage Practice: Developing Prosody

- Using the tune from *Going on a Bear Hunt*, sing or chant the "Dino Dig" call back (page 11 in the storybook) with children, echoing each line.
  We're going on a dino dig. (a dino dig, a dino dig)
  We're going to find big bones. (We're going to find big bones . . .)
- Demonstrate expressive, fluent reading of the first page. Read at a rate just slightly faster than students' rate.
  The old SUV rumbled down the highway. Benjamin Franklin . . .
- Guide practice with your voice.
  Read the paragraph with me. The old SUV rumbled down the highway. Benjamin Franklin . . .
- Provide individual turns while others track with their fingers and whisper read.
- Repeat with one paragraph at a time. Repeat steps with each remaining paragraph.

CORRECTING DECODING ERRORS

During story reading, gently correct any error, then have students reread the sentence.

REPEATED READINGS

Prosody

On the second reading, students practice developing prosody—phrasing and expression. Research has shown that prosody is related to both fluency and comprehension.

WITH THE TEACHER

Chapter 1

The E-Mail

Think about the chapter title. What do you think will happen in this chapter?[1]

The old SUV rumbled down the highway. Benjamin Franklin Thomas Edison Wright, his brother, Albert Einstein Louis Braille Wright, and his father, Dr. Wilbur Wright, were excited to be on their way.

10

MAKING CONNECTIONS

Identifying—Where; Responding

After reading the page, say something like:

It sounds like the family is going to have fun. Where are they going? (on a dino dig)

If someone asked you to go on a dino dig, what would you say?

COMPREHENDING AS YOU GO

❶ **Apply:** Predicting (Someone will send an e-mail. Someone will get an e-mail . . .)

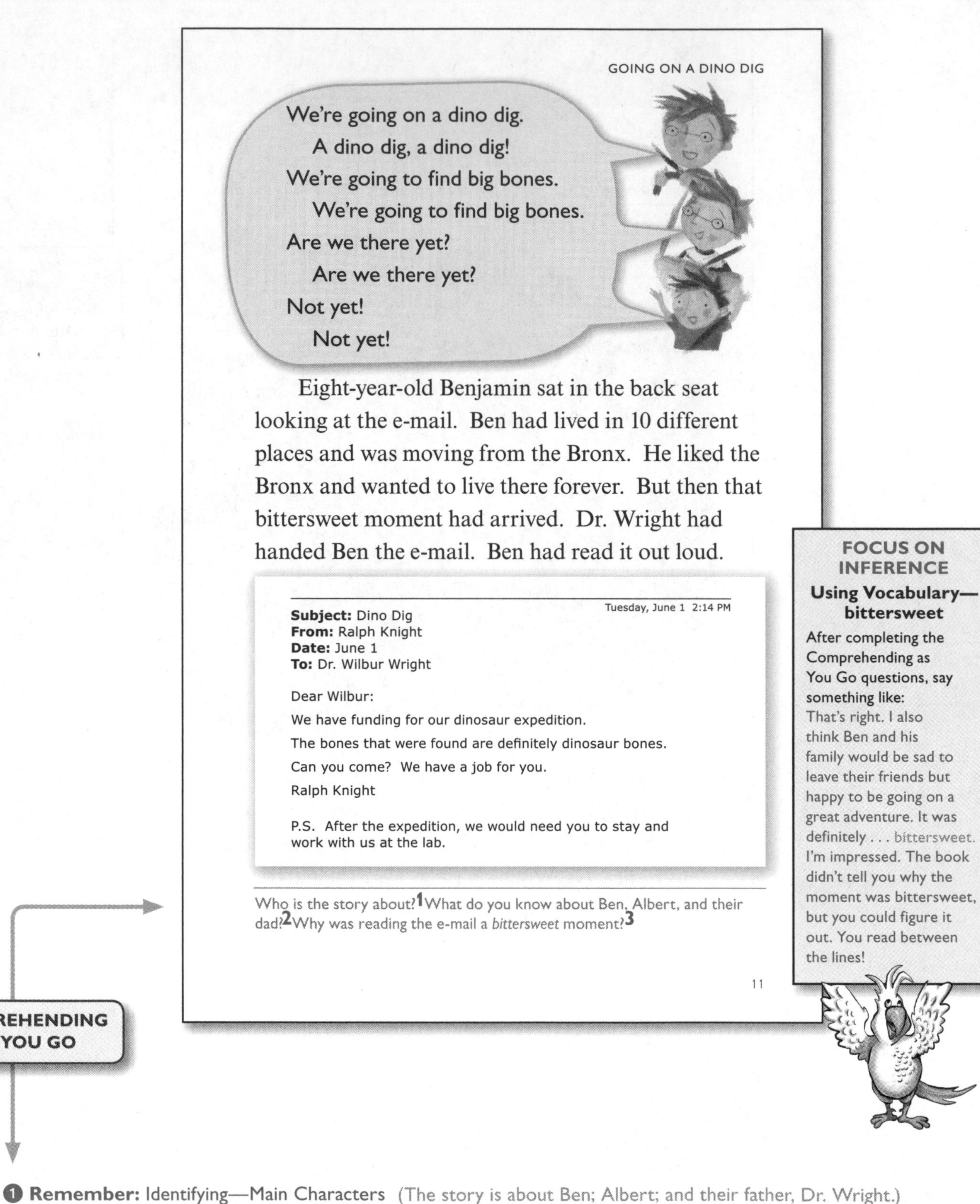

GOING ON A DINO DIG

We're going on a dino dig.
A dino dig, a dino dig!
We're going to find big bones.
We're going to find big bones.
Are we there yet?
Are we there yet?
Not yet!
Not yet!

Eight-year-old Benjamin sat in the back seat looking at the e-mail. Ben had lived in 10 different places and was moving from the Bronx. He liked the Bronx and wanted to live there forever. But then that bittersweet moment had arrived. Dr. Wright had handed Ben the e-mail. Ben had read it out loud.

Tuesday, June 1 2:14 PM

Subject: Dino Dig
From: Ralph Knight
Date: June 1
To: Dr. Wilbur Wright

Dear Wilbur:

We have funding for our dinosaur expedition.

The bones that were found are definitely dinosaur bones.

Can you come? We have a job for you.

Ralph Knight

P.S. After the expedition, we would need you to stay and work with us at the lab.

Who is the story about?[1] What do you know about Ben, Albert, and their dad?[2] Why was reading the e-mail a *bittersweet* moment?[3]

11

FOCUS ON INFERENCE

Using Vocabulary—bittersweet

After completing the Comprehending as You Go questions, say something like:
That's right. I also think Ben and his family would be sad to leave their friends but happy to be going on a great adventure. It was definitely . . . bittersweet. I'm impressed. The book didn't tell you why the moment was bittersweet, but you could figure it out. You read between the lines!

COMPREHENDING AS YOU GO

1. **Remember:** Identifying—Main Characters (The story is about Ben; Albert; and their father, Dr. Wright.)
2. **Apply:** Priming Background Knowledge (They move around a lot. They have five computers. Ben is in second grade . . .)
3. **Apply:** Inferring; **Understand:** Defining and Using Vocabulary—bittersweet (Ben is sad to leave the Bronx, but he is happy to go on a dino dig.)

WITH THE TEACHER

Albert had started jumping up and down.

Without thinking, Ben had hooted, "A dino dig! Dad, we have to go. Dino bones! Wow! It could be a T. rex or maybe even a velociraptor."

Soon the Wrights were packed and ready to move again. Traffic out of New York was terrible. It seemed like everyone was leaving the city for summer vacation.

How can you tell Albert is excited to go on a dinosaur *expedition*?[1] How can you tell Ben is excited to go on a dinosaur expedition?[2]

12

COMPREHENDING AS YOU GO

❶ **Understand:** Using Vocabulary—expedition; **Apply:** Inferring (Albert jumped up and down.)

❷ **Understand:** Using Vocabulary—expedition; **Apply:** Inferring (Ben said, "A dino dig! Dad, we have to go. Dino bones! Wow!")

Four days later, a weary Dr. Wright and his boys walked into the campsite singing:

A half-dozen worried adults were at the campsite, sipping coffee and talking. A tall thin man walked over to greet the three Wrights. He tipped his dusty hat and stuck out his hand. Dr. Wright shook the man's hand and said, "Good to see you, Ralph."

Why was Dr. Wright *weary*?[1] Who is Ralph?[2]

COMPREHENDING AS YOU GO

❶ **Apply:** Inferring; Using Vocabulary—weary (Dr. Wright was weary because he drove for four days.)

❷ **Understand:** Identifying—Who (Ralph sent the e-mail inviting them on the dino dig.)

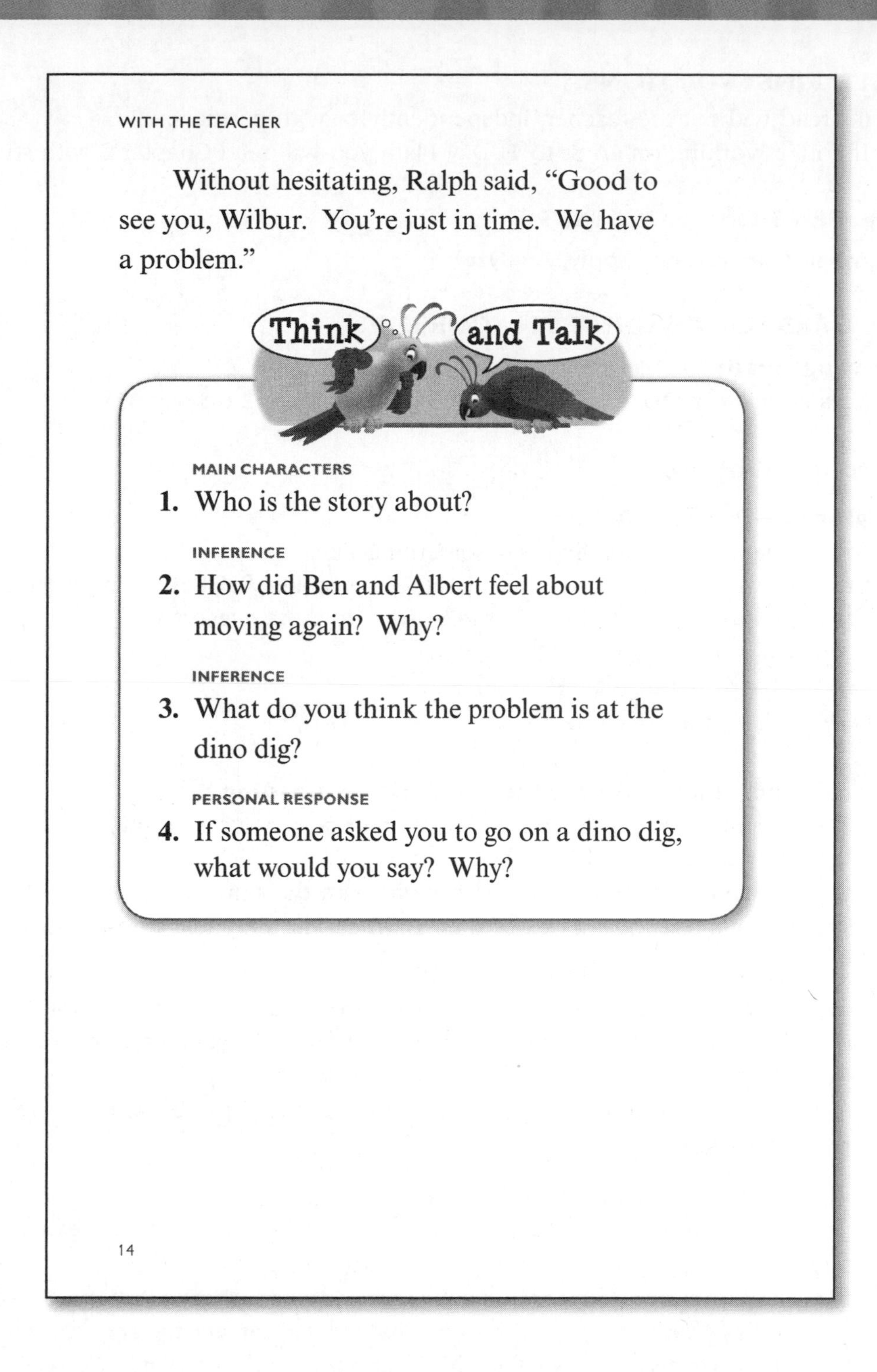

WITH THE TEACHER

Without hesitating, Ralph said, "Good to see you, Wilbur. You're just in time. We have a problem."

MAIN CHARACTERS

1. Who is the story about?

INFERENCE

2. How did Ben and Albert feel about moving again? Why?

INFERENCE

3. What do you think the problem is at the dino dig?

PERSONAL RESPONSE

4. If someone asked you to go on a dino dig, what would you say? Why?

14

❶ **Remember:** Identifying—Main Characters (The story is about Ben; his brother, Albert; and their dad.)

❷ **Apply:** Inferring; Explaining; Using Vocabulary—bittersweet (It was bittersweet for them. They were happy to go on the dino dig but sad to leave the Bronx.)

❸ **Apply:** Inferring—Problem (The expedition is not going well. They lost their gear. They can't find fossils . . .)

❹ **Evaluate:** Responding (I would say "yes." It sounds like fun. No, I don't like camping or digging in the dirt.)

CHAPTER 2 INSTRUCTIONS

Students read without the teacher, independently or with partners.
Note: If you're working on an 8- to 11-Day Plan, you will read Chapter 2 with students.

COMPREHENSION PROCESSES

Remember, Understand, Apply, Analyze

PROCEDURES FOR READING ON YOUR OWN

> **PREP NOTE**
> **Setting a Purpose**
> Write questions on a chalkboard, white board, or large piece of paper before working with your small group.

1. Getting Ready

Have students turn to "Going on a Dino Dig," Chapter 2 on page 15.

2. Setting a Purpose

Explaining—Problem, Action

Before students begin reading, say something like:
In the next pages, you are going to find out what problem Ralph is talking about and what happens to Albert. Read to find out the answers to these questions:

- What was Ralph's problem?
- What happened to Albert?
- What did Albert think he found?

3. Reading on Your Own: Partner or Whisper Reading

- Have students take turns reading every other page with a partner or have students whisper read pages 15–18 on their own.
- Continue having students track each word with their fingers.
- Have students ask themselves or their partners the gray text questions.

For Whisper Reading, say something like:
Everyone, turn to page 15. This is where you're going to start reading on your own—without me. You will whisper read as you track with your finger, so I can see where you are in your work.
Turn to page 18. That's where you are going to stop reading.
Remember to ask yourself the gray text questions. You get to be your own teacher.
Now turn back to page 15.

For Partner Reading, say something like:
Everyone, turn to page 15. This is where you're going to start Partner Reading.
Where are you going to sit? (at our desks, side by side)
You will take turns reading pages. If you are the listener, what will you do? (keep my book flat, follow with my finger, compliment my partner, ask my partner the gray text questions)
If you are the reader, what will you do? (keep my book flat, finger track, read quietly, answer the questions)
Turn to page 18. That's where you are going to stop reading.

4. Comprehension and Skill Work

For students on a 6-Day Plan, tell them they will do Comprehension and Skill Activities 1 and 2 after they read on their own. Guide practice, as needed. For teacher directions, see pages 31 and 32. (For 8- to 11-Day Plans, see the Lesson Planner, page 9.)

5. Homework 1: Repeated Reading

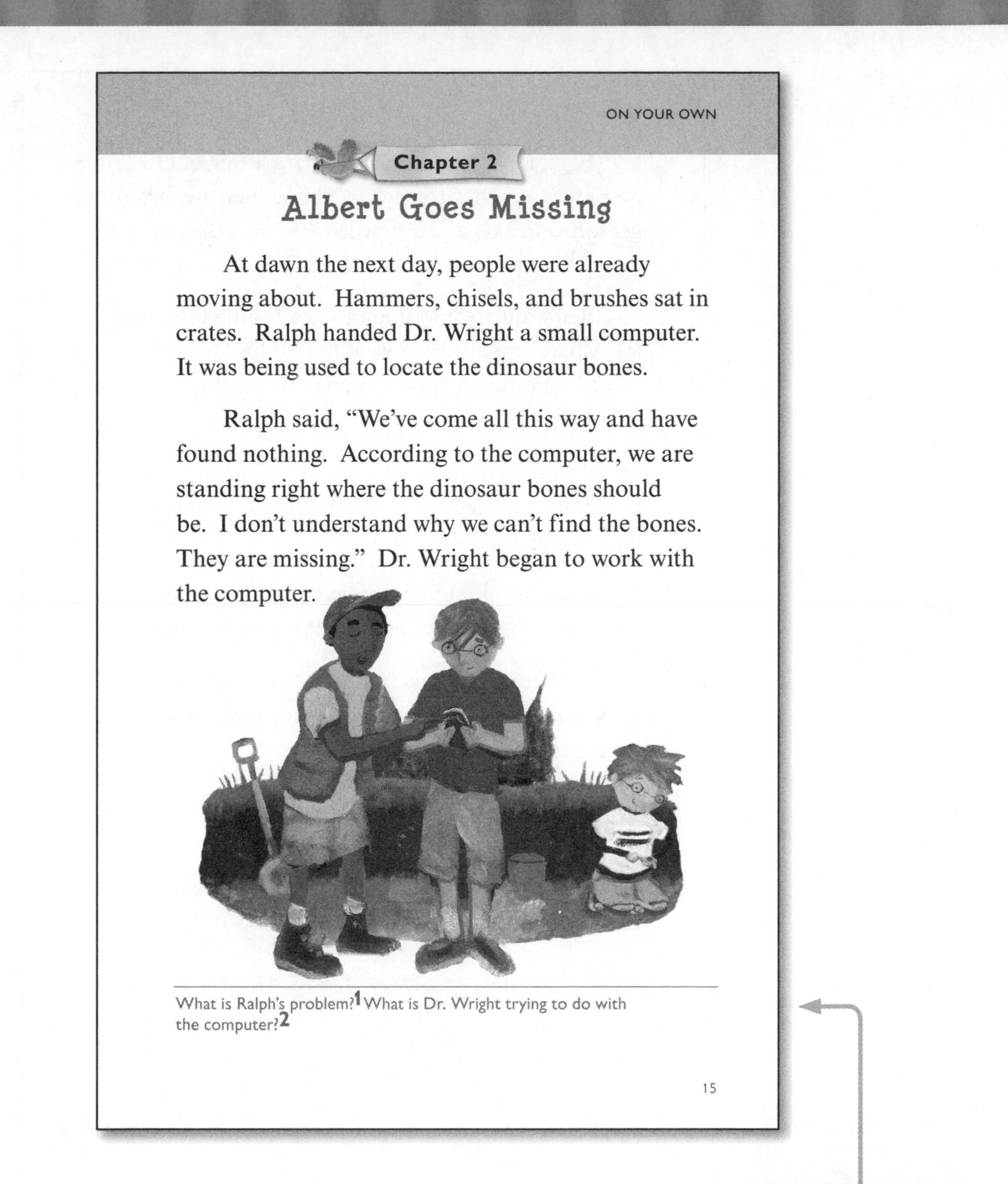

ON YOUR OWN

Chapter 2

Albert Goes Missing

At dawn the next day, people were already moving about. Hammers, chisels, and brushes sat in crates. Ralph handed Dr. Wright a small computer. It was being used to locate the dinosaur bones.

Ralph said, "We've come all this way and have found nothing. According to the computer, we are standing right where the dinosaur bones should be. I don't understand why we can't find the bones. They are missing." Dr. Wright began to work with the computer.

What is Ralph's problem?[1] What is Dr. Wright trying to do with the computer?[2]

15

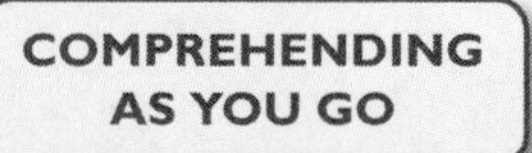

❶ **Understand:** Explaining—Problem (Ralph can't find the dinosaur bones. They are missing.)

❷ **Analyze:** Inferring; **Apply:** Explaining (Dr. Wright is trying to figure out where the bones are. He is trying to fix the computer . . .)

ON YOUR OWN

Eggs, toast, and ham slices were sitting out for everyone to grab. Stomach rumbling, Ben decided to get some breakfast. He crawled into the little pup tent to get Albert, but Albert's sleeping bag was empty.

Ben wandered around the small camp looking for Albert. Finally, Ben went to find his father. "Dad," said Ben. "Albert's gone. He must have wandered off."

Ralph organized a rescue party. Everyone was determined to find little Albert. Still, Dr. Wright looked worried.

Everyone went in different directions hollering, "Albert! Albert!" Ben and Dr. Wright went east.

An hour later, they stopped to rest. Dr. Wright leaned over the mountain stream and splashed cold water on his hot, worried face.

Suddenly, Ben said, "Dad, listen. Do you hear that?"

It was hard to hear anything but the rushing of the mountain stream. Ben yelled, "Albert!"

What is the problem?[1] Why is Dr. Wright hot and worried?[2]

16

COMPREHENDING AS YOU GO

1. **Understand:** Explaining—Problem (Albert is gone.)
2. **Apply:** Inferring, Explaining (He is hot and worried because he's been looking for Albert for a long time. He is worried that Albert might be hurt . . .)

Then Ben and Dr. Wright whooped. They could hear Albert calling, "Dad, Ben . . ."

Dr. Wright and Ben scrambled over to a huge fallen tree. They could barely see Albert's head. He stood in a small space between two huge logs. He was just too small to get out by himself.

Why hadn't Albert returned to the camp?[1]

COMPREHENDING AS YOU GO

❶ **Understand:** Explaining (Albert hadn't returned to the camp because he was stuck between two big logs.)

ON YOUR OWN

Albert's eyes kind of puddled up. As Dr. Wright reached down to pull him out, he said, "It's okay, Albert. We've got you now."

Albert hugged Dr. Wright's leg. Then he looked up and asked, "Did you see 'em?"

"See what?" asked Dr. Wright.

"The footprints," said Albert. "There were footprints. I followed them, and then I didn't know where I was."

Dr. Wright smiled. "It's okay, Albert."

Albert said, "I really mean it! Just like that boy in Canada. I found dinosaur footprints."

NOTE TO TEACHERS

The suggested Read Aloud for this unit is about a real boy who found dinosaur tracks. His discovery led to the oldest dinosaur skeleton ever found in western Canada.

Was Dr. Wright angry with Albert? Why or why not?[1] What does Albert think he found?[2]

18

COMPREHENDING AS YOU GO

❶ **Apply:** Inferring, Explaining (No, Dr. Wright was happy to find Albert. He told him it was okay . . .)

❷ **Remember:** Identifying—What (Albert thinks he found dinosaur footprints.)

STORY COMPREHENSION

COMPREHENSION PROCESSES

Remember, Apply, Evaluate

WRITING TRAITS

Word Choice
Conventions—Complete Sentence, Capital, Period, Ending Quotation Marks

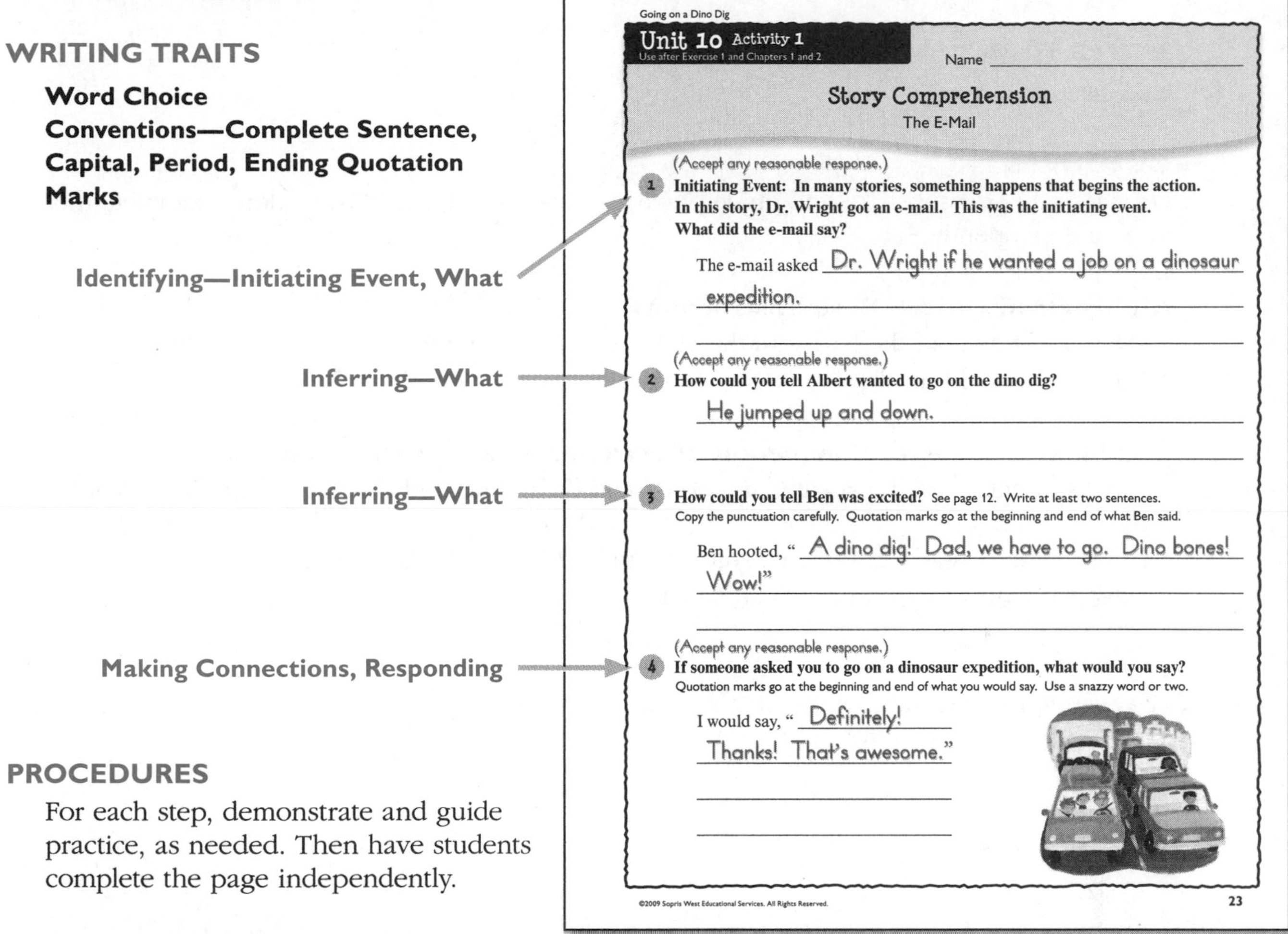

Going on a Dino Dig

Unit 10 Activity 1
Use after Exercise 1 and Chapters 1 and 2

Name ______________________

Story Comprehension
The E-Mail

Identifying—Initiating Event, What

(Accept any reasonable response.)
1. **Initiating Event: In many stories, something happens that begins the action. In this story, Dr. Wright got an e-mail. This was the initiating event. What did the e-mail say?**

The e-mail asked Dr. Wright if he wanted a job on a dinosaur expedition.

Inferring—What

(Accept any reasonable response.)
2. **How could you tell Albert wanted to go on the dino dig?**

He jumped up and down.

Inferring—What

3. **How could you tell Ben was excited?** See page 12. Write at least two sentences. Copy the punctuation carefully. Quotation marks go at the beginning and end of what Ben said.

Ben hooted, " A dino dig! Dad, we have to go. Dino bones! Wow!"

Making Connections, Responding

(Accept any reasonable response.)
4. **If someone asked you to go on a dinosaur expedition, what would you say?** Quotation marks go at the beginning and end of what you would say. Use a snazzy word or two.

I would say, " Definitely! Thanks! That's awesome."

 23

PROCEDURES

For each step, demonstrate and guide practice, as needed. Then have students complete the page independently.

Sentence Completion/Writing—Specific Instructions

- For Items 1 and 2, have students read the instructions and write a sentence or sentences. Remind them that a sentence starts with a capital and ends with a period.

★For Item 3, have students read the question and directions. Tell students they will be writing what Ben hooted or said. Have students find the beginning quotation marks that are provided. Tell students to add ending punctuation on the last sentence they write and then add the ending quotation marks.

- Have students read Item 4. Have students find the beginning quotation marks, brainstorm possible responses, and identify the appropriate punctuation. Say something like:
  What might you say if someone asked you to go on a dino dig? Try to use a snazzy word.
  (Awesome! Definitely! Incredible! . . .)
  What punctuation should go at the end of each sentence you write?
  (a period, an exclamation mark)
  Yes, an exclamation mark would be good because you would be excited.
  After the end mark in your last sentence, be sure to close with the . . . ending quotation marks.

★= New in this unit

VOCABULARY AND ALPHABETICAL ORDER

COMPREHENSION PROCESSES

Remember, Understand, Apply

WRITING TRAITS

Conventions—Period

PROCEDURES

For each step, demonstrate and guide practice, as needed. Then have students complete the page independently.

Alphabetical Order—Basic Instructions

- Have students read the letters in the alphabet column and fill in the missing letters.
- Have students fill in the blanks for the vocabulary words in the column.

Vocabulary: Sentence Completion, Illustrating—Basic Instructions

- Have students read the vocabulary words and definitions and fill in any blanks to complete the definitions.
- Have students read the sample sentences and fill in the blanks.
- Have students visualize and illustrate each sentence.

Self-monitoring

Have students check and correct their work.

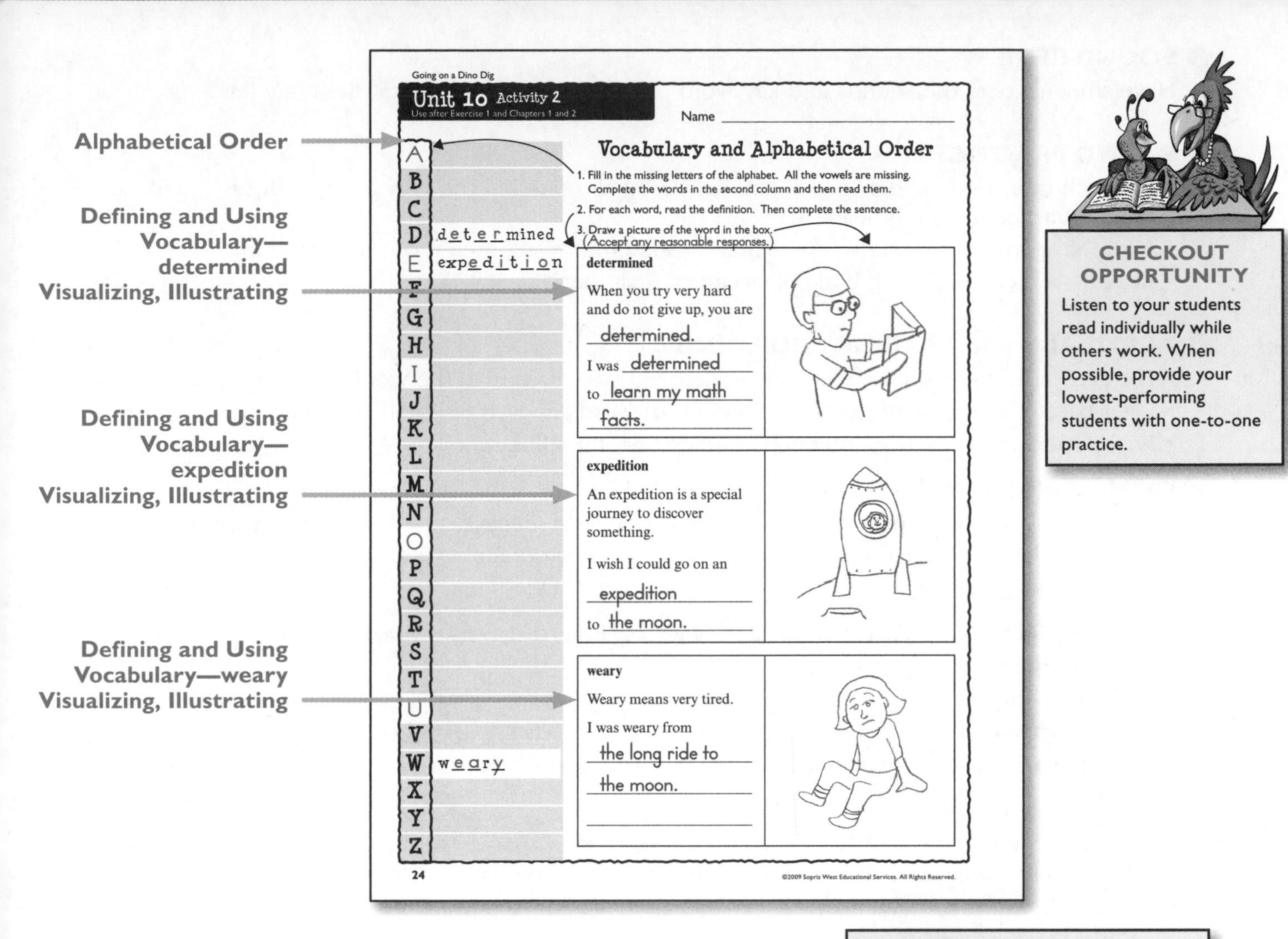

CHECKOUT OPPORTUNITY

Listen to your students read individually while others work. When possible, provide your lowest-performing students with one-to-one practice.

BUILDING INDEPENDENCE

Principles of Instruction

For each step, demonstrate and guide practice only as needed.

- **Demonstrate:** Have students orally answer the items while you demonstrate how to complete the page.
- **Guide:** Have students orally answer the items, but do not demonstrate how to complete the page.
- **Independent With Support:** Have students silently read over the items and ask any questions they may have.

❶ SOUND REVIEW

Have students read the sounds and key word phrases. Work for accuracy, then fluency.

❷ SOUND PRACTICE

- For each task, have students spell and say the focus sound in the gray bar. For Bossy E and Mixed Practice, read the headers.
- Next, have students read each underlined sound, the word, then the whole column.
- Repeat with each column, building accuracy first, then fluency.

❸ ACCURACY AND FLUENCY BUILDING

- For each task, have students say any underlined part, then read the word.
- Set a pace. Then have students read the whole words in each task and column.
- Provide repeated practice, building accuracy first, then fluency.

C1. Multisyllabic Words

- For the list of words divided by syllables, have students read each syllable, then the whole word. Use the word in a sentence, as appropriate.
- For the list of whole words, build accuracy and then fluency.

perfect There wasn't a thing wrong. Everything was . . . *perfect.*
moment Let's rest for a . . . *moment.*
Tuesday The day after Monday is . . . *Tuesday.*
herbivores Animals that eat only plants are called . . . *herbivores.*
carnivores Animals that eat mostly meat are called . . . *carnivores.*

D1. Tricky Words

- For each Tricky Word, have students use the sounds and word parts they know to silently sound out the word. Use the word in a sentence to help with pronunciation.
- If the word is unfamiliar, tell students the word.

field
Look at the first word. Sound out the word silently. Thumbs up when you know the word.
What's the word? (field) The farmer plowed his . . . *field.*
Read the word three times. (field, field, field)

uncovered We could smell the luscious soup when the cook . . . *uncovered* . . . the pot.
fours My baby brother crawled on all . . . *fours.*
once The trick was so hard she could do it only . . . *once.*
heard The sneeze was so loud that everybody . . . *heard* . . . it.
watched I climbed the tree as my dog sat below and . . . *watched.*

- Have students go back and read the whole words in the column.

❹ WORDS IN CONTEXT

Tell students to use the sounds and word parts they know to silently sound out the word. Then have students read the sentence. Assist, as needed.

❺ MORPHOGRAPHS AND AFFIXES

6 DINOSAUR WORDS

- Remind students they will be reading dinosaur names or words related to dinosaurs.
- Have students read each word, using the pronunciation guide for help.
- Use each word in a sentence.

Going on a Dino Dig

Unit 10 Exercise 2

Use before Chapter 3

1. SOUND REVIEW Have students review sounds for accuracy, then for fluency.

A	a as in ago	-y as in baby	ge as in page	oa as in boat	ue as in blue
B	kn	ci	ph	ou	ew

2. SOUND PRACTICE In each column, have students spell and say the sound, then say any underlined sound and the word. Next, have students read the whole column.

oa	Bossy E	aw	Mixed Practice
groan float croak	saved smiled bones	dawn crawled yee-haw	ground stood clears

3. ACCURACY AND FLUENCY BUILDING For each column, have students say any underlined part, then read each word. Next, have students read the whole column.

A1 Compound Words	B1 Word Endings	C1 Multisyllabic Words		D1 Tricky Words
riverbank	roots	per•fect	perfect	field
everyone	prints	mo•ment	moment	uncovered
everywhere	crouched	Tues•day	Tuesday	fours
understand	hunting	her•bi•vores	herbivores	once
	whispered	car•ni•vores	carnivores	heard
	insisted			watched

4. WORDS IN CONTEXT For each word, have students use the sounds and word parts they know to figure out the word. Then have them read the sentences.

A	di•no•saur	Do you think it would be safe to have a dinosaur as a pet?
B	bu•sy	I had so much to do. I was very busy.
C	de•ter•mined	Bob trained all week for the race. Bob was determined to win.

5. MORPHOGRAPHS AND AFFIXES Have students read each underlined word part, then the word.

A	likable	finally	comfortable	rerun
B	decide	expedition	undo	belong

6. DINOSAUR WORDS Have students use the sounds and word parts they know and the pronunciation guide to read the words.

theropods	thir-uh-pods	ornithopods	or-nith-uh-pods

18

BUILDING MASTERY WITH JAZZY PRACTICE (Reminder)

For variety, practice underlined sounds in a jazzy rhythm. Say something like:

Listen to me do Sound Practice in a rhythm. I'm going to quickly say each underlined sound two times and then read the word.
/ō/, /ō/, groan;
/ō/, /ō/, float;
/ō/, /ō/, croak.

Your turn. Start at the top of the first column and keep going.
/ō/, /ō/, groan;
/ō/, /ō/, float;
/ō/, /ō/, croak.

COMPREHENSION PROCESSES

Understand, Apply

PROCEDURES

1. Introducing Vocabulary

hesitate ★insist ★crouch ★save the day, expedition

- For each vocabulary word, have students read the word by parts, then read the whole word.
- Read the student-friendly explanations to students as they follow with their fingers. Then have students use the vocabulary word by following the gray text.
- Review and discuss the photos and illustrations.

USING VOCABULARY

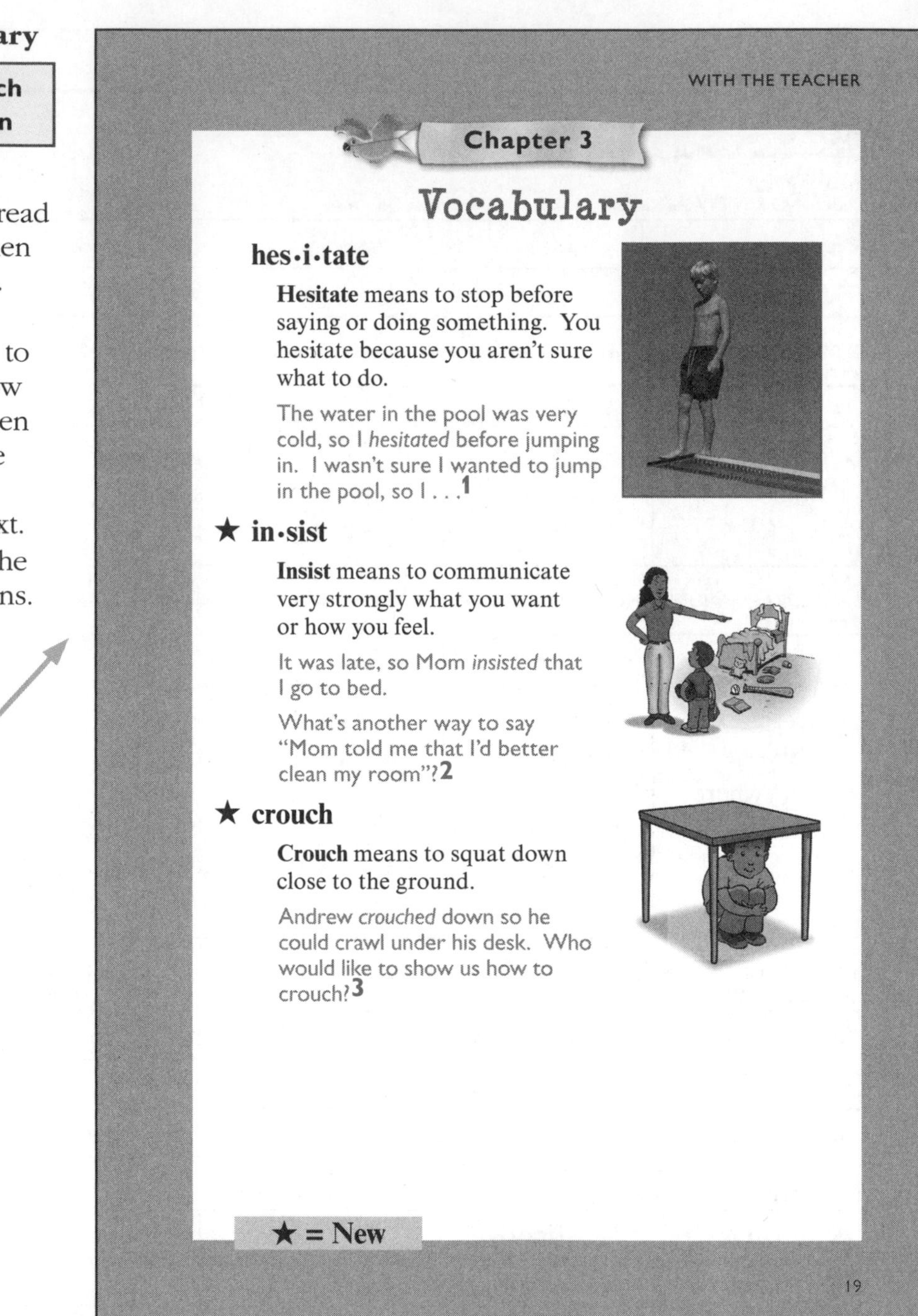

❶ **Understand:** Using Vocabulary—hesitate (hesitated)

❷ **Understand:** Using Vocabulary—insist (Mom insisted that I clean my room.)

❸ **Apply:** Demonstrating; Using Vocabulary—crouch

DEMONSTRATE

Using Vocabulary—crouch

Have one student model for your group, or model how to crouch yourself.

★= New in this unit

2. **Now You Try It!**
   - Read or paraphrase the directions.
   - For each word, have students read the word by parts, then read the whole word.
   - Have students explain or define the word in their own words. Say something like:
     Look at the word. Say the parts, then read the whole word.
     (ex•pe•di•tion, expedition)
     Now, let's pretend that we're going to explain or define the word *expedition* to a friend. [Sam], what would you say?
     Start with "An *expedition* is . . . " (An expedition is a special trip to look for something.)
     That's right. An expedition is a special trip or journey to look for or discover something.
   - Have students turn to the appropriate page in the glossary and discuss how their definitions are the same as or different from the glossary's. Your students may like their definitions better.

Note: By defining a word in their own words, students are demonstrating depth of word knowledge. Verbatim responses demonstrate memorization only. Encourage paraphrasing.

❶ **Apply:** Using Vocabulary—save the day (Someone could go get the bat and ball and save the day.)

❷ **Understand:** Using Vocabulary—expedition (An expedition is a special journey to study or discover something.)

CHAPTER 3 INSTRUCTIONS

Students read Chapter 3 with the teacher.

COMPREHENSION PROCESSES

Understand, Apply, Analyze

PROCEDURES

1. Reviewing Chapters 1 and 2

Identifying—Problem, Events, What

- Have students turn to page 10. Quickly review the main characters.
- Have students turn to page 15. Quickly review what happened to Albert. Discuss the questions from Setting a Purpose.
  Say something like:
  Yesterday, you read Chapter 2 on your own. Let's see what you found out.
  What was Ralph's problem? (They couldn't find the dinosaur bones.)
  What happened to Albert? (Albert wandered off and got stuck between two big logs.)
  What did Albert think he found? (He thought he found dinosaur tracks.)

2. Introducing Chapter 3

Identifying—Title; Predicting

Discuss the title. Say something like:
What's the title of this chapter? (Chip, Chip, Dig, Dig)
Why do you think this chapter is called "Chip, Chip, Dig, Dig"?

3. First Reading

- Ask questions and discuss the story as indicated by the gray text.
- Mix group and individual turns, independent of your voice.
  Have students work toward a group accuracy goal of 0–2 errors.
  Quietly keep track of errors made by all students in the group.
- After reading the story, practice any difficult words.
  Reread the story if students have not reached the accuracy goal.

4. Second Reading, Timed Readings: Repeated Reading

- As time allows, have students do Timed Readings while others follow along.
- Time individuals for 30 seconds and encourage each child to work for a personal best.
- Determine words correct per minute. Record student scores.

5. Partner or Whisper Reading: Repeated Reading

Before beginning independent work, have students finger track and partner or whisper read.

6. Comprehension and Skill Work

Tell students they will do Comprehension and Skill Activities 3 and 4 after they read Chapter 3. Guide practice, as needed. (For teacher directions, see pages 43 and 44.)

7. Homework 2: Repeated Reading

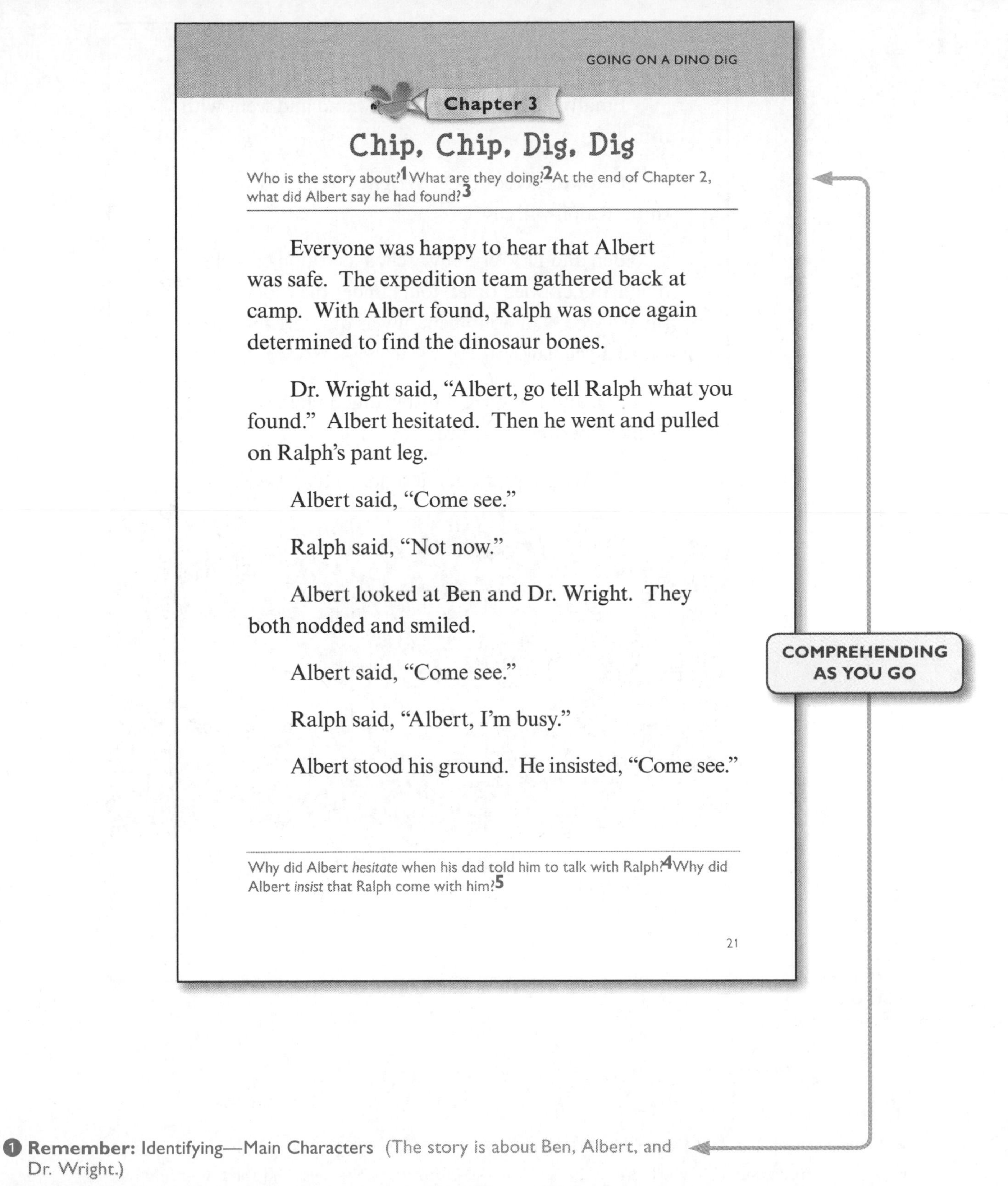

1. **Remember:** Identifying—Main Characters (The story is about Ben, Albert, and Dr. Wright.)
2. **Remember:** Identifying—What (They are looking for dinosaur bones.)
3. **Remember:** Identifying—What (Albert said he had found dinosaur footprints.)
4. **Apply:** Inferring; Using Vocabulary—hesitate (Albert wasn't sure what to say to Ralph. Albert was scared of Ralph . . .)
5. **Apply:** Inferring; Using Vocabulary—insist (Albert knew he had found something important. He wanted to show Ralph the footprints.)

WITH THE TEACHER

Finally, Ralph took Albert's hand and went with him.

Ben whispered to Dr. Wright, "What do you think Ralph will say?"

Ben and Dr. Wright watched as Ralph crouched down and crawled on all fours under the roots of the big tree. For a moment, it was quiet. Then they heard a yee haw!

Ben and Dr. Wright just grinned. Ben said, "I think Albert has saved the day."

Dr. Wright said, "Kind of looks that way."

Look at the picture. Describe what is happening.[1] What do you think will happen next?[2]

22

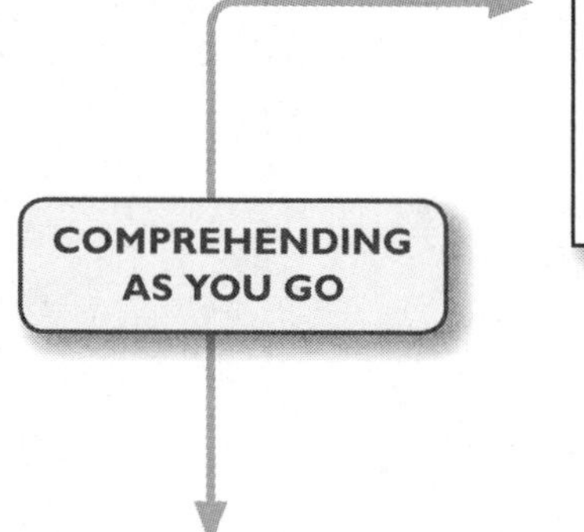

❶ **Understand:** Viewing, Describing (Ralph is crawling under the tree to look at the dinosaur footprints.)

❷ **Apply:** Predicting (They will dig for bones near the footprints. They will find the bones and put them together to make a dinosaur skeleton . . .)

FOCUS ON INFERENCE: READING BETWEEN THE LINES

Inferring; Using Idioms and Expressions—save the day; Looking Back

After completing the page, say something like:
The story makes us feel like Albert must have found dinosaur tracks. Let's see if we can figure out why it seems that way. What did Ralph yell?
(yee haw)
What do you think he's saying? (He's excited.)
Wonderful. What would make Ralph that excited? (dino tracks)

You are reading between the lines. I think you are right.

What do you think Albert found? (dinosaur tracks)

There's one other clue on page 22 that makes us think Albert found real dino tracks. Look back in your book. What is that clue? (Ben said, "I think Albert has saved the day.")

Special Note: Have students read Ben's field log to themselves. Say something like: Look at the field log that Ben kept. It's really cool. Read Ben's field log. When you're done, look up and we'll talk about what they found on the dino dig.

BEN'S FIELD LOG	
Tuesday, June 15	–Albert leads team to prints under fallen tree. –Team clears fallen trees from riverbank. a. 123 prints uncovered b. 28 prints belong to carnivores (theropods, T. rex?) c. 95 prints belong to herbivores (ornithopods) –Ralph thinks T. rex may have been hunting the ornithopods. –Perfect or what?

Think and Talk

INFERENCE

1. How did Albert save the day?

SUMMARIZATION

2. What did you learn from Ben's field log?

❶ **Apply:** Inferring; Using Idioms and Expressions—save the day (He saved the day by finding the dinosaur fossils they were looking for.)

❷ **Understand:** Summarizing (They found 123 footprints. Twenty-eight of the footprints belong to carnivores. Ninety-five prints belong to herbivores . . .)

STORY COMPREHENSION • MAZE READING

COMPREHENSION PROCESSES

Remember, Understand

WRITING TRAITS

Conventions—Complete Sentence, Capital, Period

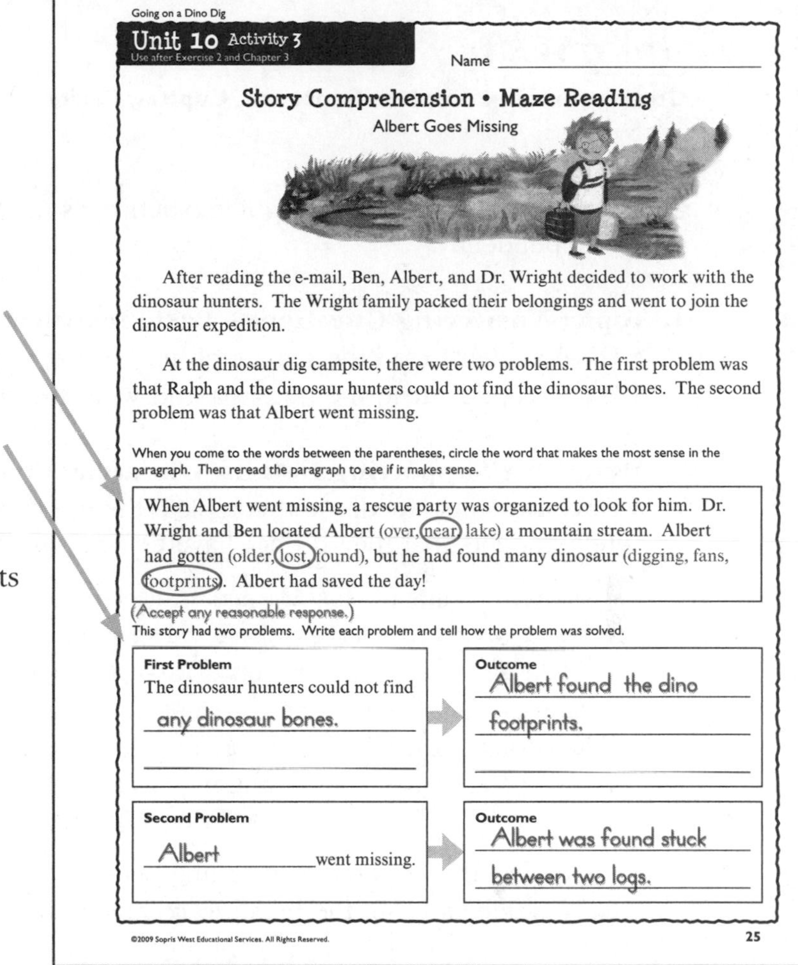

Going on a Dino Dig

Unit 10 Activity 3
Use after Exercise 2 and Chapter 3

Name ____________________

Story Comprehension • Maze Reading

Albert Goes Missing

After reading the e-mail, Ben, Albert, and Dr. Wright decided to work with the dinosaur hunters. The Wright family packed their belongings and went to join the dinosaur expedition.

At the dinosaur dig campsite, there were two problems. The first problem was that Ralph and the dinosaur hunters could not find the dinosaur bones. The second problem was that Albert went missing.

When you come to the words between the parentheses, circle the word that makes the most sense in the paragraph. Then reread the paragraph to see if it makes sense.

When Albert went missing, a rescue party was organized to look for him. Dr. Wright and Ben located Albert (over, near, lake) a mountain stream. Albert had gotten (older, lost, found), but he had found many dinosaur (digging, fans, footprints). Albert had saved the day!

(Accept any reasonable response.)

This story had two problems. Write each problem and tell how the problem was solved.

First Problem		Outcome
The dinosaur hunters could not find any dinosaur bones.	→	Albert found the dino footprints.
Second Problem		**Outcome**
Albert went missing.	→	Albert was found stuck between two logs.

©2009 Sopris West Educational Services. All Rights Reserved. 25

Comprehension Monitoring, Test Taking

Using Graphic Organizer
Identifying—Problems
Explaining—Outcome; Sequencing

PROCEDURES

For each step, demonstrate and guide practice, as needed. Then have students complete the page independently.

1. Maze Reading—Specific Instructions

- Tell students that the paragraphs retell the story. Have students read the first two paragraphs.
- Review directions for completing a Maze Reading. Say something like:

  The third paragraph is a Maze Reading exercise. Remember, a maze is like a puzzle. You will choose the correct word to complete the sentence. Read and stop at the parentheses. (When Albert went missing, a rescue party . . .)
  There are three choices. Try reading the whole sentence with the first word choice.
  (Dr. Wright and Ben located Albert . . . *over* a mountain stream.)
  Does "over a mountain stream" make sense? (no)
  No. That is not correct. Try the next word.
  (Dr. Wright and Ben located Albert . . . *near* a mountain stream.)
  Does that make sense? (yes)
  Reread the sentence to yourself with the word *near*.
  If it makes sense, circle the word *near*. If you aren't sure, try the last word.
  When you are done, reread the whole paragraph. Ask yourself if it makes sense.

2. Problem/Outcome: Sequence Chart—Basic Instructions

- Have students read the directions and sentence starters in the first column of boxes, then fill in the blanks to identify each problem.
- Have students write complete sentences to explain how each problem was resolved.
- Think aloud with students and brainstorm possible answers, as needed. Remind them to look back in their books or at the paragraph if they need help.

MAIN IDEA AND SUPPORTING DETAILS

COMPREHENSION PROCESSES

Remember, Understand

WRITING TRAITS

Conventions—Complete Sentence, Capital, Period

PROCEDURES

For each step, demonstrate and guide practice, as needed. Then have students complete the page independently.

1. Topic: Answering Questions—Basic Instructions (Item 1)

- Have students read the paragraph in the box.
- Have students read the question and write the correct answer in the blank.

2. Main Idea/Supporting Details: Hierarchy Chart—Specific Instructions (Item 2)

- Have students identify and complete the graphic organizer with three supporting details. Tell students that they do not have to write in complete sentences. Say something like:

  Read Item 2. (Supporting Details: The search party looked for Albert . . .)
  You will write three places where the search party looked for Albert.
  These are the supporting details that tell where the search party looked for Albert.
  What's one place where the search party looked? (They searched around the campsite.)
  Take a look at the first box. It has a bullet before the words *around the* . . .
  To complete this graphic organizer, you can write a phrase. You don't have to write a complete sentence. So you can finish the phrase with *campsite*.

- Repeat for the next two supporting details.
- Have students fill in the blank to complete the main idea.

3. Main Idea: Sentence Writing, Illustrating—Basic Instructions (Item 3)

Have students write the main idea sentence. Remind them to use a capital and a period. Then have students visualize and illustrate the main idea.

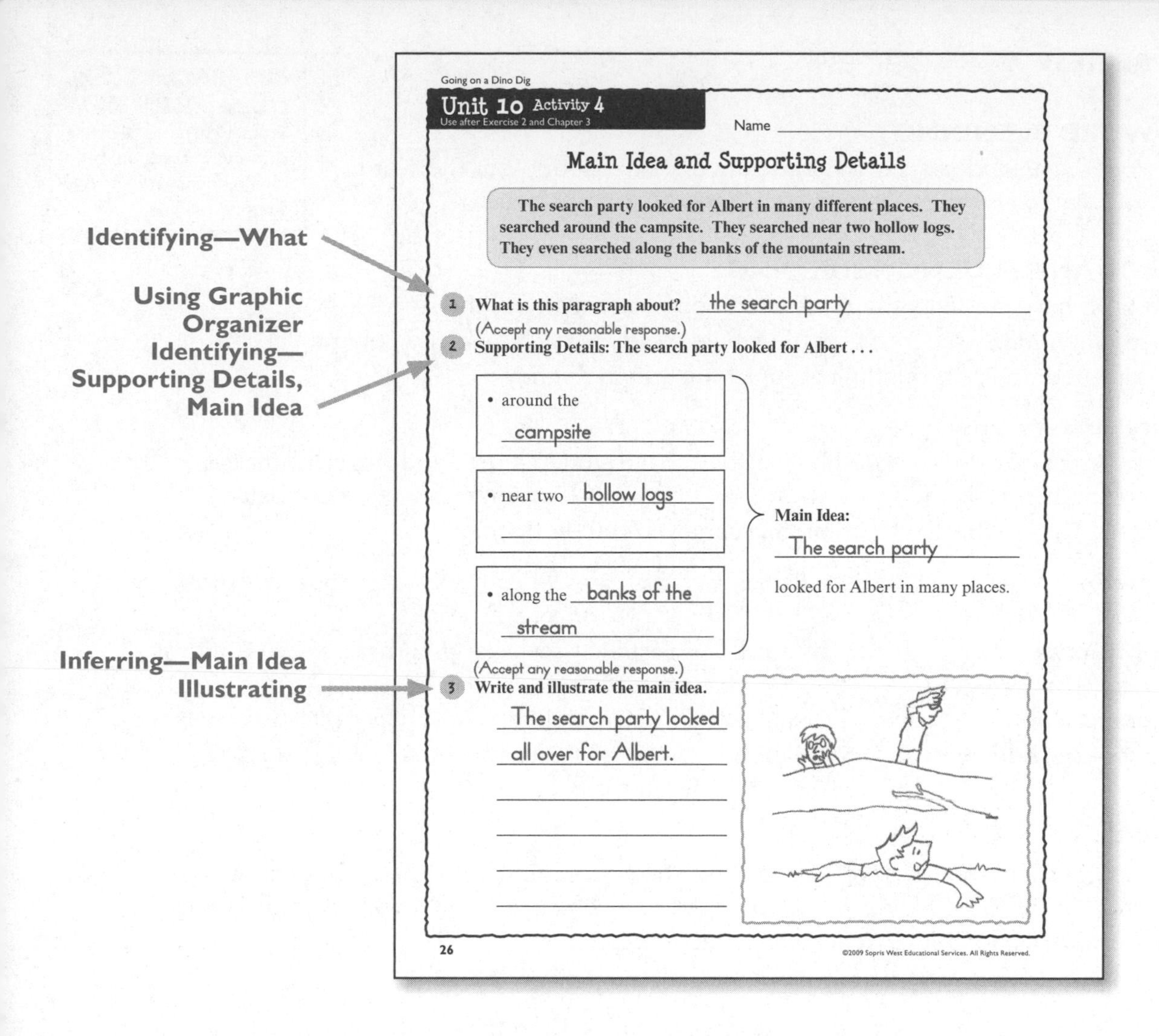
Identifying—What
Using Graphic Organizer Identifying—Supporting Details, Main Idea
Inferring—Main Idea Illustrating
Going on a Dino Dig
Unit 10 Activity 4
Use after Exercise 2 and Chapter 3
Name
Main Idea and Supporting Details
The search party looked for Albert in many different places. They searched around the campsite. They searched near two hollow logs. They even searched along the banks of the mountain stream.
1 What is this paragraph about? the search party
(Accept any reasonable response.)
2 Supporting Details: The search party looked for Albert . . .
• around the campsite
• near two hollow logs
• along the banks of the stream
Main Idea:
The search party
looked for Albert in many places.
(Accept any reasonable response.)
3 Write and illustrate the main idea.
The search party looked all over for Albert.
26
©2009 Sopris West Educational Services. All Rights Reserved.

❶ SOUND REVIEW

> **PACING**
> Exercise 3a should take about 10 minutes, allowing about 10 minutes for the Fact Summary Focus Lesson.

❷ SHIFTY WORD BLENDING

For each word, have students say the underlined sound, sound out the word smoothly, and say it. Use the words in sentences, as appropriate.

❸ ACCURACY AND FLUENCY BUILDING

- For each task, have students say any underlined part, then read the word.
- Set a pace. Then have students read the whole words in each task and column.
- Provide repeated practice, building accuracy first, then fluency.

D1. Multisyllabic Words

- For the list of words divided by syllables, have students read and finger count each syllable, then read the whole word. Use the word in a sentence, as appropriate.
- For the list of whole words, build accuracy and then fluency.

timeline	2 syllables	The dates when the events happened were shown on a . . . *timeline.*
continents	3 syllables	Earth has seven large land masses, or . . . *continents.*
Antarctica	4 syllables	The South Pole is in . . . *Antarctica.*
saber-toothed tiger	5 syllables	A kind of tiger that lived long ago was the . . . *saber-toothed tiger.*

E1. Tricky Words

- For each Tricky Word, have students use the sounds and word parts they know to silently sound out the word. Use the word in a sentence to help with pronunciation.
- If the word is unfamiliar, tell students the word.

break

Look at the first word. This word rhymes with *steak*. Read the word. (break)

The workers were tired and needed a . . . *break.*

Read the word three times. (break, break, break)

died

Look at the next word. Thumbs up when you know the word.

When winter came, the flowers . . . *died.* Read the word two times. (died, died)

period	Many different dinosaurs lived during the Jurassic . . . *period.*
oceans	The Pacific and the Atlantic are names of . . . *oceans.*
weighed	I got on the scale so I could be . . . *weighed.*
human	I am a . . . *human.*

- Have students go back and read the whole words in the column.

❹ DINOSAUR WORDS

- Have students read each word, using the pronunciation guide for help.
- Use the words in sentences, as needed.

❺ GENERALIZATION: READING NEW WORDS IN PARAGRAPHS

- Have students read the paragraph silently, then out loud. Tell students to use the sounds and word parts they know to read any difficult words.
- Repeat practice, as needed.

A Dinosaur Timeline

Unit 10 Exercise 3a

Use before Chapter 1

1. SOUND REVIEW Use selected Sound Cards from Units 1–10.

2. SHIFTY WORD BLENDING For each word, have students say the underlined part, sound out smoothly, then read the word.

egg	edge	ledge	let	left

3. ACCURACY AND FLUENCY BUILDING For each column, have students say any underlined part, then read each word. Next, have students read the whole column.

A1 New Sound Practice	B1 Mixed Practice	C1 Word Endings	D1 Multisyllabic Words	E1 Tricky Words
moan	clue	building	time•line	break
coast	grew	taller	con•ti•nents	died
boast	number	largest	Ant•arc•ti•ca	period
roamed	notes	include	sa•ber-toothed ti•ger	oceans
A2 Mixed Practice	**B2** Affixes	including	timeline	weighed
place	behind	**C2** Buildups	continents	human
apart	below	appear	Antarctica	
drift	before	appeared	saber-toothed tiger	
topic	freely	disappeared		
tracks				

4. DINOSAUR WORDS Have students use the sounds and word parts they know and the pronunciation guide to read the words.

A	Argentinosaurus	Are-jen-teen-uh-sore-us
B	Brachiosaurus	Brak-ee-uh-sore-us
C	Plateosaurus	Plat-ee-uh-sore-us
D	Tyrannosaurus rex	Tuh-ran-uh-sore-us rex
E	Pangaea	Pan-jee-uh

5. GENERALIZATION Have students read the paragraph silently, then out loud. (New words: research, enormous, extinct)

When I grow up, I want to be a scientist who does research on dinosaurs. I want to learn more about these enormous creatures that are now extinct. I might even be able to discover a new dinosaur. That would be super!

APPROPRIATE CORRECTIONS (Reminder)

Write any difficult words on a board or clipboard.

Single-Syllable Pattern Words

Have students identify the difficult sound, then sound out and say the word.

Multisyllabic Words

Draw loops under each word part and then guide practice with your hand.

Tricky Words

Have students sound out or read the word by parts, then say the word. Next have students say, spell, and say the word.

After gently correcting a word with the group, go on to other tasks or words. Return to the difficult word at least three times.

EXERCISE 3b (Focus Lesson)

FACT SUMMARY

FOCUS LESSON
Skills and Strategies

> **PREP NOTES**
> To demonstrate how to write a fact summary, use an overhead of page 20 in student *Exercise Book 2,* write on a transparency placed over the page, or use a paper copy.

> **PACING**
> Exercise 3b should take about 10 minutes.

PURPOSE

The purpose of this lesson is to provide explicit instruction in how to use notes to write a fact summary. The lesson prepares students for Comprehension and Skill Work. Students do not write in their books.

COMPREHENSION PROCESSES

Remember, Understand, Create

PROCEDURES

❶ INTRODUCTION

Identifying—Topic, Fact; Generating Ideas

Explain the purpose of the lesson. Say something like:

A fact summary is a great strategy for remembering and understanding interesting information. Look at your Focus Lesson. It shows Ben's research notes. What was his topic? (Dinosaurs Lived Long Ago) What were the facts Ben listed about dinosaurs? Everyone, read the facts. They . . . (lived on Earth before people . . .)

❷ WRITING A FACT SUMMARY

Identifying—Topic, What, Fact; Generating Ideas

- Introduce topic sentences. Say something like:

  Once you've identified a topic and taken notes, you're ready to write a fact summary.
  What was Ben's topic? (Dinosaurs Lived Long Ago)
  The first sentence of a fact summary paragraph is a topic sentence.
  A topic sentence tells what the paragraph is going to be about.
  What does the topic sentence tell us? (what the paragraph is going to be about)

  Everyone, read the topic sentence. (Dinosaurs ruled Earth long, long ago.)
  That's a great topic sentence. It tells us what the paragraph will . . . (be about).
  The writer also used the snazzier word *ruled* instead of *lived.*
  What did the author write to emphasize how long ago? (long, long ago)

- Demonstrate and guide writing the first fact.

  Now we need to write facts about the topic. Read the first fact. (lived on Earth before . . .)
  Let's turn the fact into a sentence. We're going to start with "They."
  We could write, "They lived on Earth before there were people."
  We could also write a more interesting sentence by adding details or using snazzier words.
  We could write "They lived on Earth for *millions of years* before there were people.
  After the word "They," write "lived on Earth for millions of years before there were people."

- Have students brainstorm a second sentence, then demonstrate writing a sentence.

  What's the second fact? (left behind fossils)
  Partner 1, tell your partner a snazzy sentence using the fact "left behind fossils."

  After about minute, have Partner 2 generate a sentence.
  Then say: What are some sentences you talked about with your partner? (Dinosaurs left behind huge fossils . . .)

- Repeat with the third fact.

A Dinosaur Timeline

Unit 10 Exercise 3b (Focus Lesson)
Use after Exercise 3a and before Chapter 3

FOCUS LESSON
Skills and Strategies

STOP
Don't write in your Exercise Book.

Fact Summary

Notes About Dinosaurs

Topic: lived long ago

Fact 1: lived on Earth before people

Fact 2: left behind fossils

Fact 3: lived on Earth for 165 million years

Dinosaurs ruled Earth long, long ago.

Fact 1: They lived on Earth millions of years before there were people.

Fact 2: We know about dinosaurs because they left behind huge fossils.

Fact 3: The dinosaurs lived on Earth for 165 million years before they became extinct.

COMPREHENSION PROCESSES

Remember, Understand, Apply, Create

PROCEDURES

1. Reviewing the Table of Contents

Using Table of Contents

Have students find the Table of Contents and the title page for "A Dinosaur Timeline." Next, have students turn to page 25.

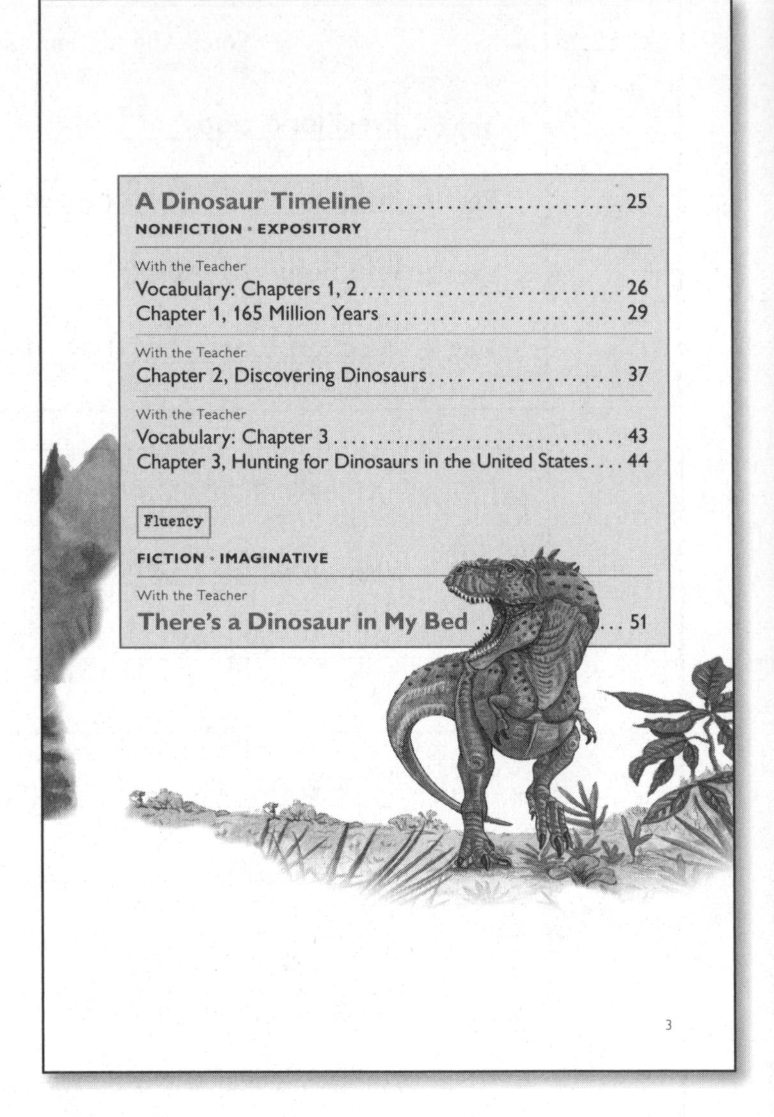

2. Introducing the Title Page and Story

Viewing; Identifying—Title, Authors, Topic, Genre; Inferring; Explaining

- Tell students the title of their new story.
  Say something like:
  Everyone, look at page 25.
  The title of the story is "A Dinosaur Timeline."
  What's the title of this story? (A Dinosaur Timeline)
  What is this story about? (dinosaurs)
- Have students identify the topic and discuss the genre.
  The first story we read was fiction.
  This story is full of facts about dinosaurs.
  We call this type of story *nonfiction.*
  What's a story called when it's made up of facts? (nonfiction)
- Introduce the authors.
  Who are the authors? (Ann Watanabe and Marilyn Sprick)
  Ms. Watanabe and Mrs. Sprick enjoyed writing this story.
  They think dinosaurs are amazing.

  The authors had fun learning new things when they researched the topic. They especially enjoyed learning about the Bone Wars. What do you think that might be about?
- Discuss the gray text questions under the picture.

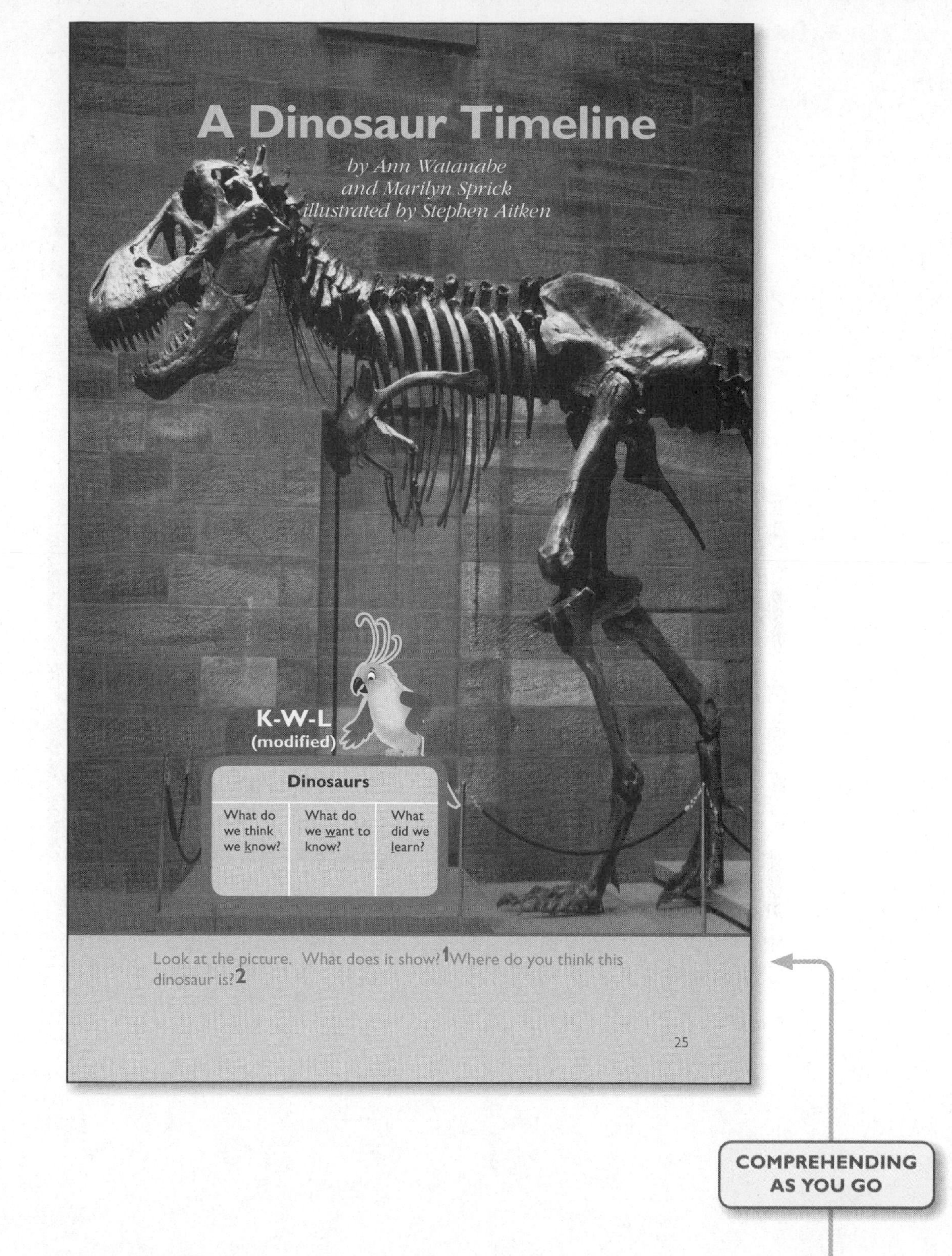

❶ **Apply:** Viewing, Inferring, Explaining (It shows a dinosaur skeleton.)

❷ **Apply:** Viewing, Inferring (It's in a museum.)

Note: See page 52 for K-W-L instructions.

3. Using K-W-L (modified)

Using Graphic Organizer, Priming Background Knowledge, Generating Ideas, Asking Questions

- Use chart paper or three columns on a chalkboard to make a K-W-L Chart.
- Demonstrate and explain that it's okay to make corrections in our knowledge. Then have students identify what they think they know about dinosaurs. Say something like:

  Reading nonfiction is always fun. Sometimes we learn new facts that make us change the way we think about things. I think dinosaurs are reptiles. I'm going to write that on the board. What do you think you already know about dinosaurs?

Dinosaurs

What do we think we know?	What do we want to know?	What did we learn?
reptiles (Ms. Mak) extinct (Ron) enormous (Andy) live on land (Jill) some fly (Lynn)	How long did dinosaurs live on Earth? (Ms. Mak) What did they eat? (Lynn) Are they herbivores, carnivores, or omnivores? (Carlos)	

- Think aloud as you demonstrate how to ask questions. Then have students generate questions about dinosaurs. Say something like:

  I wonder how long dinosaurs lived on Earth. I've heard that they lived on Earth for millions of years. My question is, "How long did dinosaurs live on Earth?"

COMPREHENSION PROCESSES

Understand, Apply

PROCEDURES

1. Introducing Vocabulary

imagine ★extinct ★roam ★fascinate ★remains ★fossil ★realize, vast

- For each vocabulary word, have students read the word by parts, then read the whole word.
- Read the student-friendly explanations to students as they follow with their fingers. Then have students use the vocabulary word by following the gray text.
- Review and discuss the photos and illustrations.

USING VOCABULARY

WITH THE TEACHER

Chapters 1, 2

Vocabulary

i·ma·gine

Imagine means to make a picture of something in your mind. You can also imagine how something might smell, taste, and feel.

Imagine life without cars. How would you get from place to place?1

★ **ex·tinct**

Extinct means died out. Animals and plants that are extinct are no longer found on Earth.

Are there any dinosaurs on Earth today? Why not?2

★ **roam**

Roam means to wander or walk around freely.

What's another way to say "Dinosaurs walked around Earth for millions of years"?3

★ = New

26

❶ **Understand:** Visualizing; Using Vocabulary—imagine (I imagine that people would ride their bikes. Someone might invent another way to get around.)

❷ **Understand:** Explaining; Using Vocabulary—extinct (There are no dinosaurs on Earth today because they are extinct.)

❸ **Understand:** Using Vocabulary—roam (Dinosaurs roamed the Earth for millions of years.)

★= New in this unit

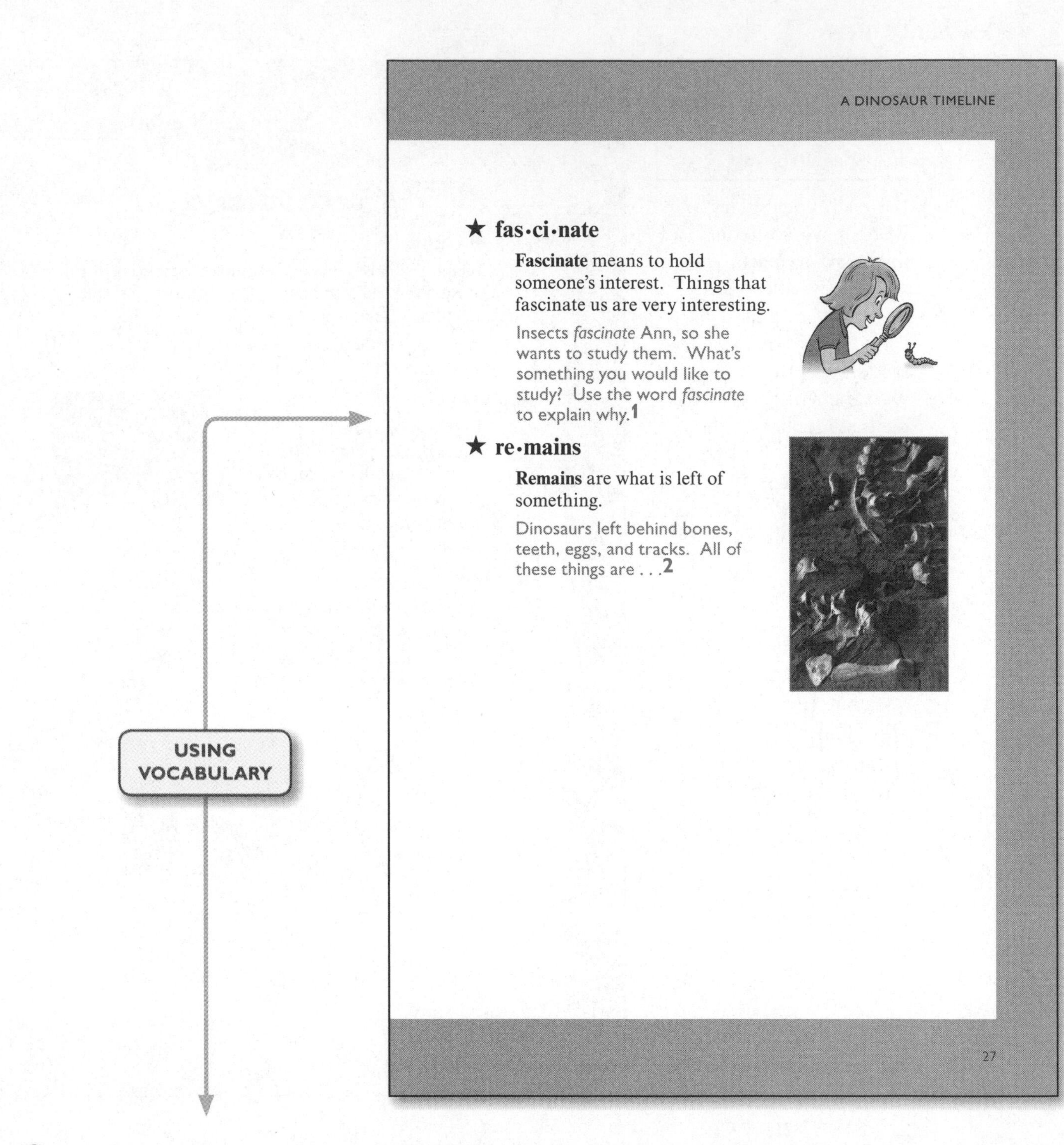

A DINOSAUR TIMELINE

★ **fas•ci•nate**

Fascinate means to hold someone's interest. Things that fascinate us are very interesting.

Insects *fascinate* Ann, so she wants to study them. What's something you would like to study? Use the word *fascinate* to explain why.**1**

★ **re•mains**

Remains are what is left of something.

Dinosaurs left behind bones, teeth, eggs, and tracks. All of these things are . . .**2**

27

❶ **Apply:** Using Vocabulary—fascinate (I would like to study horses because they fascinate me.)

❷ **Understand:** Using Vocabulary—remains (remains)

2. Now You Try It!

- Read or paraphrase the directions.
- For each word, have students read the word by parts, then read the whole word.
- Have students explain or define the word in their own words. Say something like:

  Look at the word. Read the whole word. (vast)

  Now let's pretend that we're going to explain or define the word *vast* to a friend. [Owen], what would you say?

  Start with "*Vast* is another word for . . . " (Vast is another word for huge.)

  That's right. Something vast is huge. Outer space is vast.
- Have students turn to the appropriate page in the glossary and discuss how their definitions are the same as or different from the glossary's. Your students may like their definitions better.

Note: By defining a word in their own words, students are demonstrating depth of word knowledge. Verbatim responses demonstrate memorization only. Encourage paraphrasing.

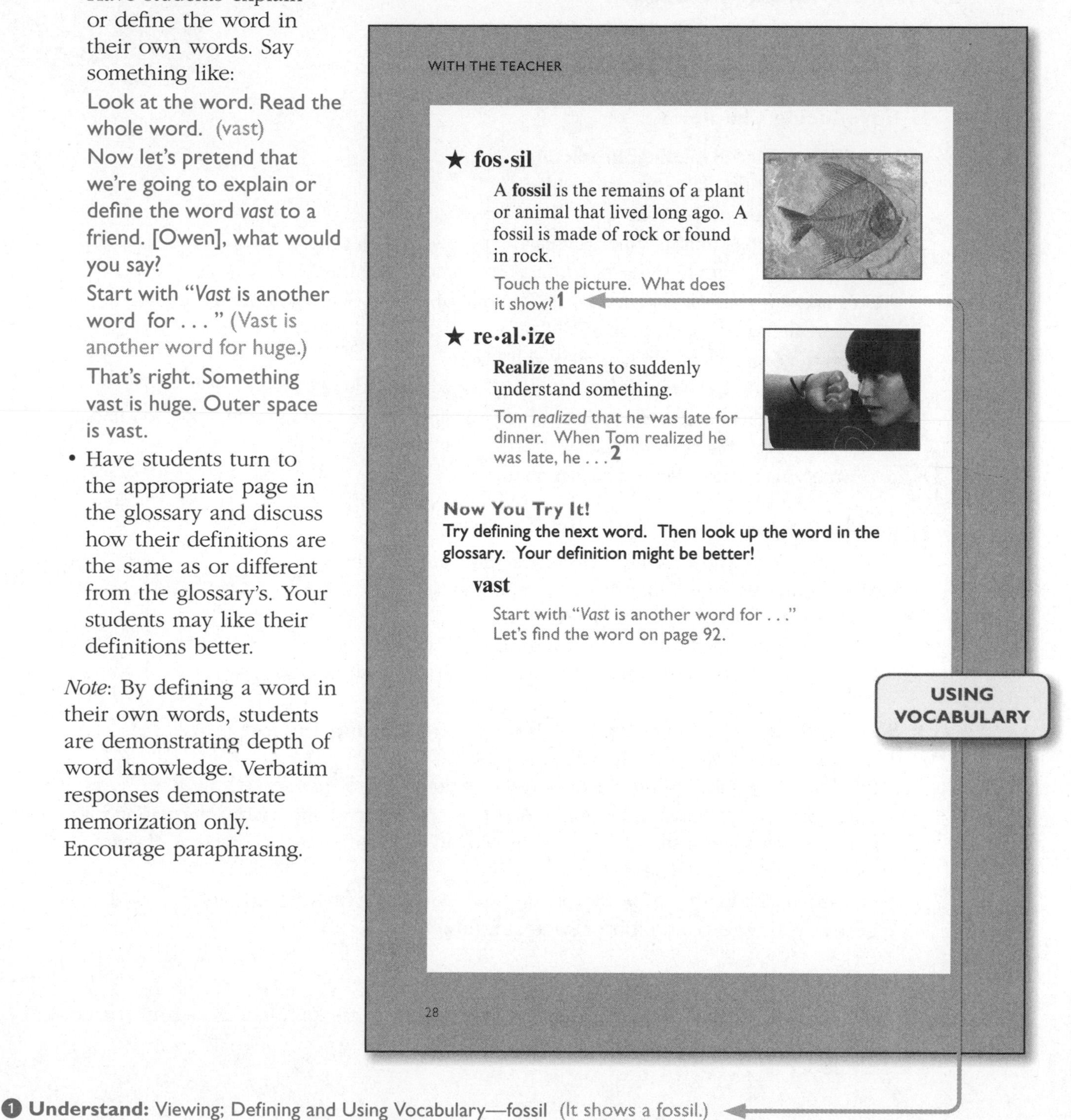

WITH THE TEACHER

★ **fos•sil**

A **fossil** is the remains of a plant or animal that lived long ago. A fossil is made of rock or found in rock.

Touch the picture. What does it show? 1

★ **re•al•ize**

Realize means to suddenly understand something.

Tom *realized* that he was late for dinner. When Tom realized he was late, he . . . 2

Now You Try It!

Try defining the next word. Then look up the word in the glossary. Your definition might be better!

vast

Start with "*Vast* is another word for . . ."
Let's find the word on page 92.

28

USING VOCABULARY

❶ **Understand:** Viewing; Defining and Using Vocabulary—fossil (It shows a fossil.)

❷ **Apply:** Using Vocabulary—realize (started to run)

CHAPTER 1 INSTRUCTIONS

Students read Chapter 1 with the teacher.

COMPREHENSION PROCESSES

Remember, Understand, Apply, Analyze, Create

PROCEDURES

1. Introducing Chapter 1

Identifying—Title, Heading; Predicting

- Discuss the title. Say something like:
  What's the title of this chapter? (165 Million Years Ago)
  That's how long dinosaurs lived on Earth. It is a very long time.
- Have students preview the headings. Say something like:
  Let's preview the headings so we can find out what we will learn about dinosaurs.
  Find the first heading on page 30. What does it say? (Dinosaurs Lived Long Ago)
  That's the topic. What do you think you'll learn?
  (What it was like when the dinosaurs lived, how long ago they lived . . .)
  Find the next heading in this chapter. Put your finger under the heading when you find it.
  Everyone, read the second heading. (Earth When Dinosaurs Lived)
  What else are you going to find out about? (We're going to find out what Earth was like . . .)

2. First Reading

- Ask questions and discuss the story as indicated by the gray text.
- Mix group and individual turns, independent of your voice.
  Have students work toward a group accuracy goal of 0–4 errors.
- After reading the story, practice any difficult words.
  Reread the story if students have not reached the accuracy goal.

CORRECTING DECODING ERRORS

During story reading, gently correct any error, then have students reread the sentence.

3. Second Reading, Short Passage Practice: Developing Prosody

- Demonstrate expressive, fluent reading of the first paragraph.
  Read at a rate just slightly faster than the students' rate. Say something like:
  Listen to my expression as I read the first page. I'm going to emphasize information that I think is interesting and the sentence that ends with an exclamation mark. "Millions of years . . . "
- Guide practice with your voice.
- Provide individual turns while others track with their fingers and whisper read.
- Repeat with one paragraph or page at a time.

4. Partner or Whisper Reading: Repeated Reading

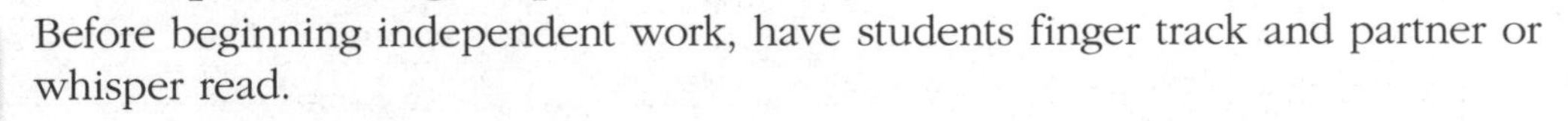

Before beginning independent work, have students finger track and partner or whisper read.

5. Comprehension and Skill Work

Tell students they will do Comprehension and Skill Activities 5 and 6 after they read Chapter 1. Guide practice, as needed. (For teacher directions, see pages 65 and 66.)

6. Homework 3: Repeated Reading

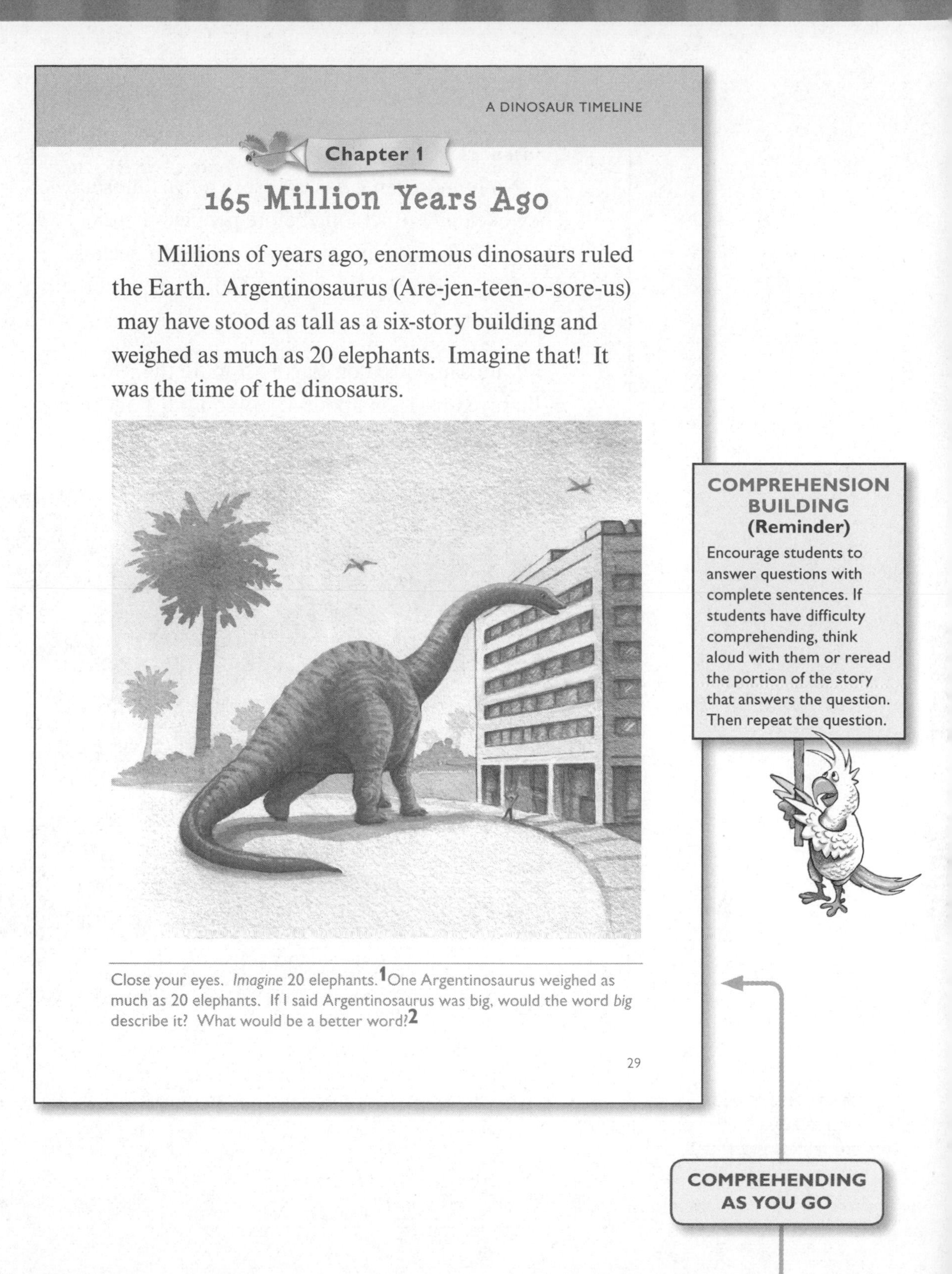

A DINOSAUR TIMELINE

Chapter 1

165 Million Years Ago

Millions of years ago, enormous dinosaurs ruled the Earth. Argentinosaurus (Are-jen-teen-o-sore-us) may have stood as tall as a six-story building and weighed as much as 20 elephants. Imagine that! It was the time of the dinosaurs.

Close your eyes. *Imagine* 20 elephants.[1] One Argentinosaurus weighed as much as 20 elephants. If I said Argentinosaurus was big, would the word *big* describe it? What would be a better word?[2]

29

COMPREHENSION BUILDING (Reminder)

Encourage students to answer questions with complete sentences. If students have difficulty comprehending, think aloud with them or reread the portion of the story that answers the question. Then repeat the question.

COMPREHENDING AS YOU GO

❶ **Understand:** Visualizing

❷ **Create:** Generating Ideas (A better word would be huge, gigantic, enormous . . .)

WITH THE TEACHER

Dinosaurs Lived Long Ago

No human being has ever seen a live dinosaur. They became extinct long before people were on Earth. We know dinosaurs lived on Earth because they left behind their eggs, their footprints, and their huge bones.

Dinosaurs lived on Earth for more than 165 million years. Then about 65 million years ago, they disappeared.

What will you learn in this section?**1** Has any person ever seen a living dinosaur? Why not?**2** How do we know about dinosaurs?**3**

30

COMPREHENDING AS YOU GO

❶ **Understand:** Inferring (We will learn when dinosaurs lived . . .)

❷ **Understand:** Explaining; Using Vocabulary—extinct (No. Dinosaurs became extinct before people were on Earth.)

❸ **Understand:** Explaining (We know about dinosaurs because they left behind eggs, footprints, and bones.)

Where do you think Ben found the facts for his notes?**1** What facts did he write down?**2** What question does Ben's research notes answer?**3**

31

TOPIC

Explain to students that the topic is what something is about. Ben's Topic 1 is like a header.

COMPREHENDING AS YOU GO

❶ **Apply:** Inferring; Explaining (He found them in this book. He went to the library . . .)

❷ **Understand:** Summarizing—Facts (Dinosaurs lived on Earth for 165 million years. Dinosaurs left behind fossils. Dinosaurs lived on Earth long before people.)

❸ **Apply:** Asking Questions; Explaining—Topic (Ben's notes answer the question, "When did dinosaurs live?")

WITH THE TEACHER

A timeline helps us understand when things happened. Look at the timeline below. It shows when the first dinosaurs appeared and when they died out. Can you find when people first appeared on Earth?

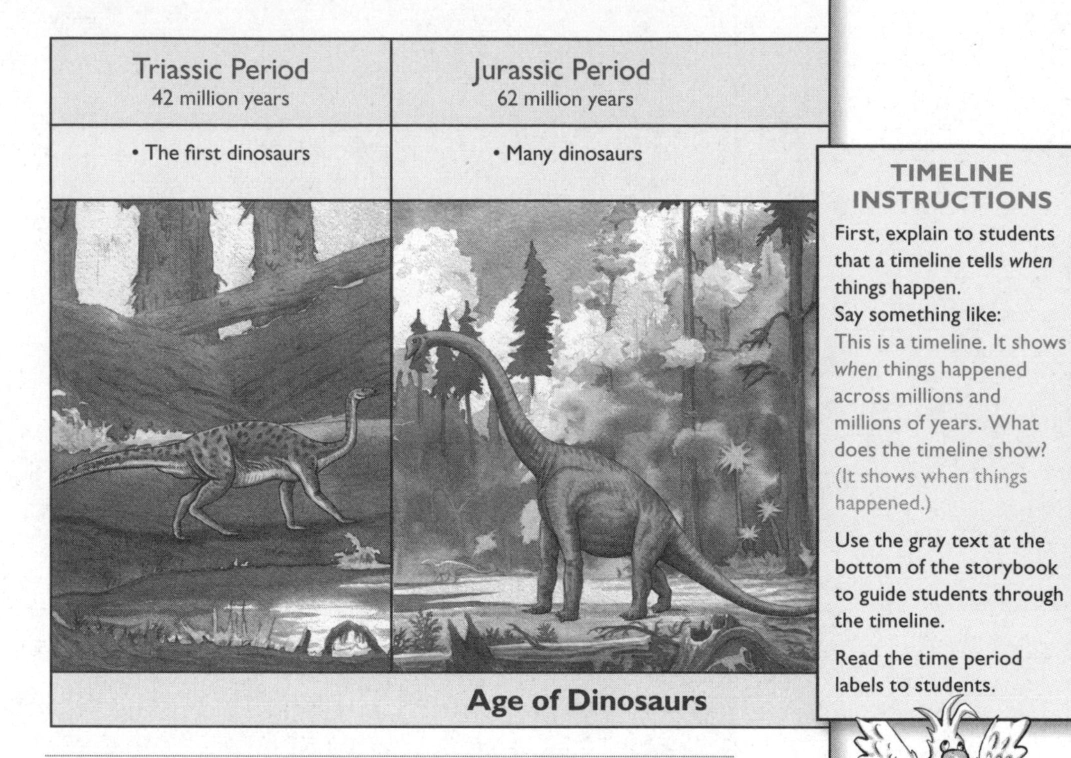

TIMELINE INSTRUCTIONS

First, explain to students that a timeline tells *when* things happen.

Say something like:
This is a timeline. It shows *when* things happened across millions and millions of years. What does the timeline show? (It shows when things happened.)

Use the gray text at the bottom of the storybook to guide students through the timeline.

Read the time period labels to students.

Touch the first box. This tells about the Triassic period. The Triassic period lasted 42 million years. Read the words next to the dot. What happened in the Triassic period?[1]

Touch the next box. This is the Jurassic period. What does the timeline tell you about dinosaurs in that time?[2]

32

COMPREHENDING AS YOU GO

1. **Understand:** Locating Information; **Remember:** Identifying—Fact (The first dinosaurs lived during this period.)
2. **Understand:** Locating Information; **Remember:** Identifying—Fact (There were many dinosaurs on Earth.)

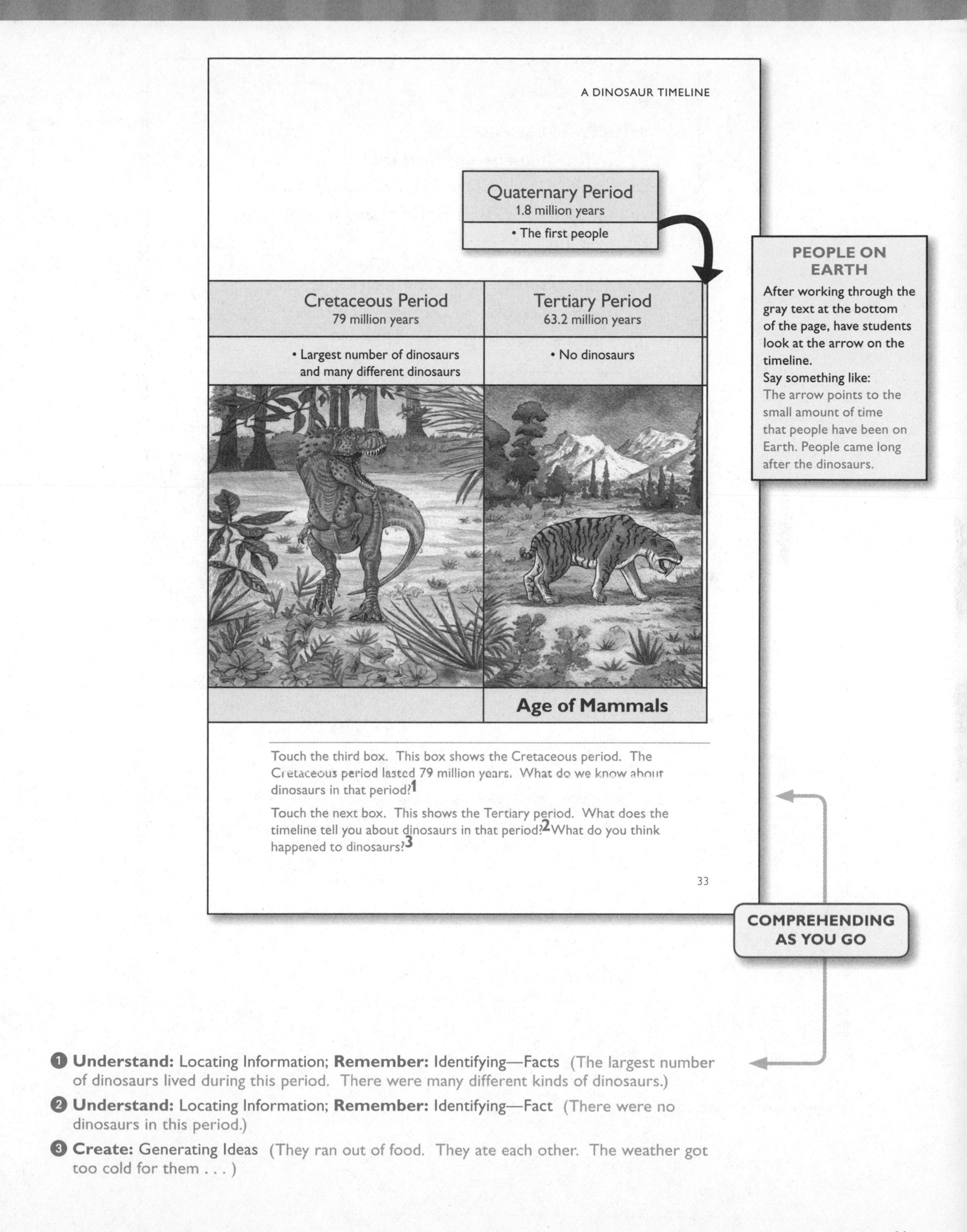

Touch the third box. This box shows the Cretaceous period. The Cretaceous period lasted 79 million years. What do we know about dinosaurs in that period?[1]

Touch the next box. This shows the Tertiary period. What does the timeline tell you about dinosaurs in that period?[2] What do you think happened to dinosaurs?[3]

PEOPLE ON EARTH

After working through the gray text at the bottom of the page, have students look at the arrow on the timeline.
Say something like:
The arrow points to the small amount of time that people have been on Earth. People came long after the dinosaurs.

COMPREHENDING AS YOU GO

1. **Understand:** Locating Information; **Remember:** Identifying—Facts (The largest number of dinosaurs lived during this period. There were many different kinds of dinosaurs.)
2. **Understand:** Locating Information; **Remember:** Identifying—Fact (There were no dinosaurs in this period.)
3. **Create:** Generating Ideas (They ran out of food. They ate each other. The weather got too cold for them . . .)

WITH THE TEACHER

Earth When Dinosaurs Lived

When dinosaurs first roamed Earth, it was a very different place than we know today. Scientists call the land where the first dinosaurs lived Pangaea (Pan-jee-uh).

Pangaea was a super continent—one vast continent. There were no oceans to cross, so dinosaurs walked freely everywhere.

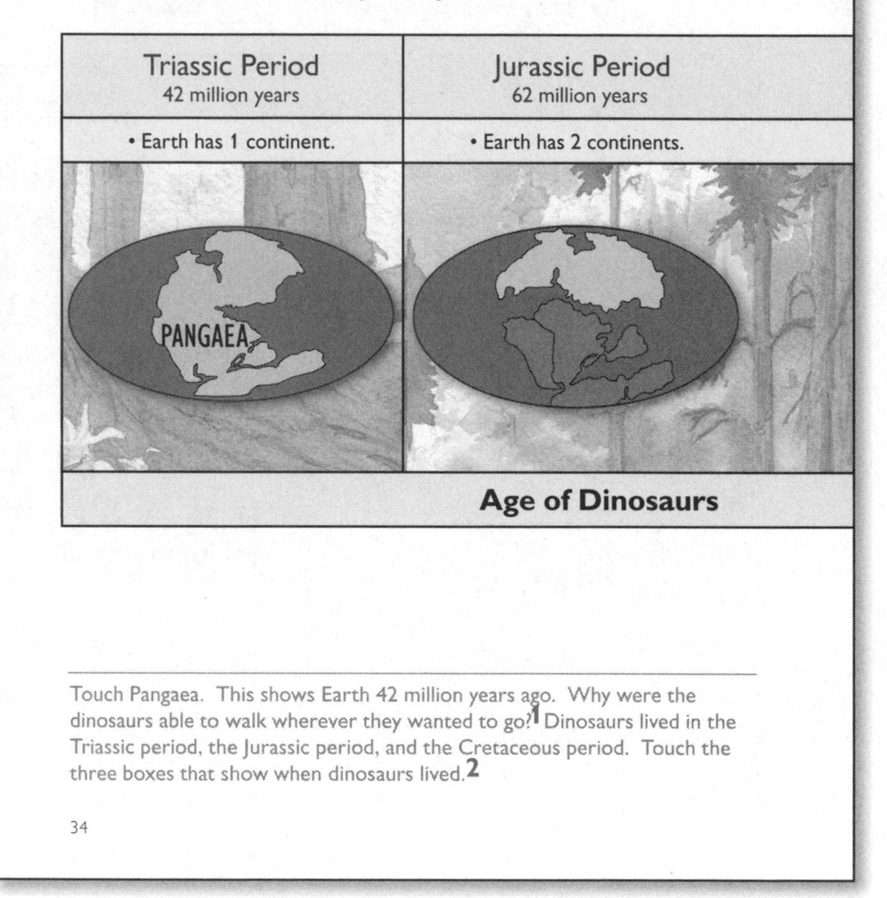

Touch Pangaea. This shows Earth 42 million years ago. Why were the dinosaurs able to walk wherever they wanted to go?[1] Dinosaurs lived in the Triassic period, the Jurassic period, and the Cretaceous period. Touch the three boxes that show when dinosaurs lived.[2]

34

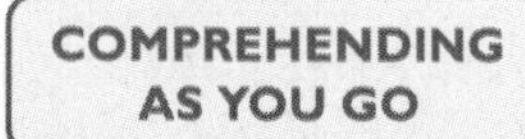

❶ **Understand:** Locating Information; Explaining (The dinosaurs walked wherever they wanted to go because Pangaea was one big continent. There were no oceans to cross.)

❷ **Understand:** Locating Information

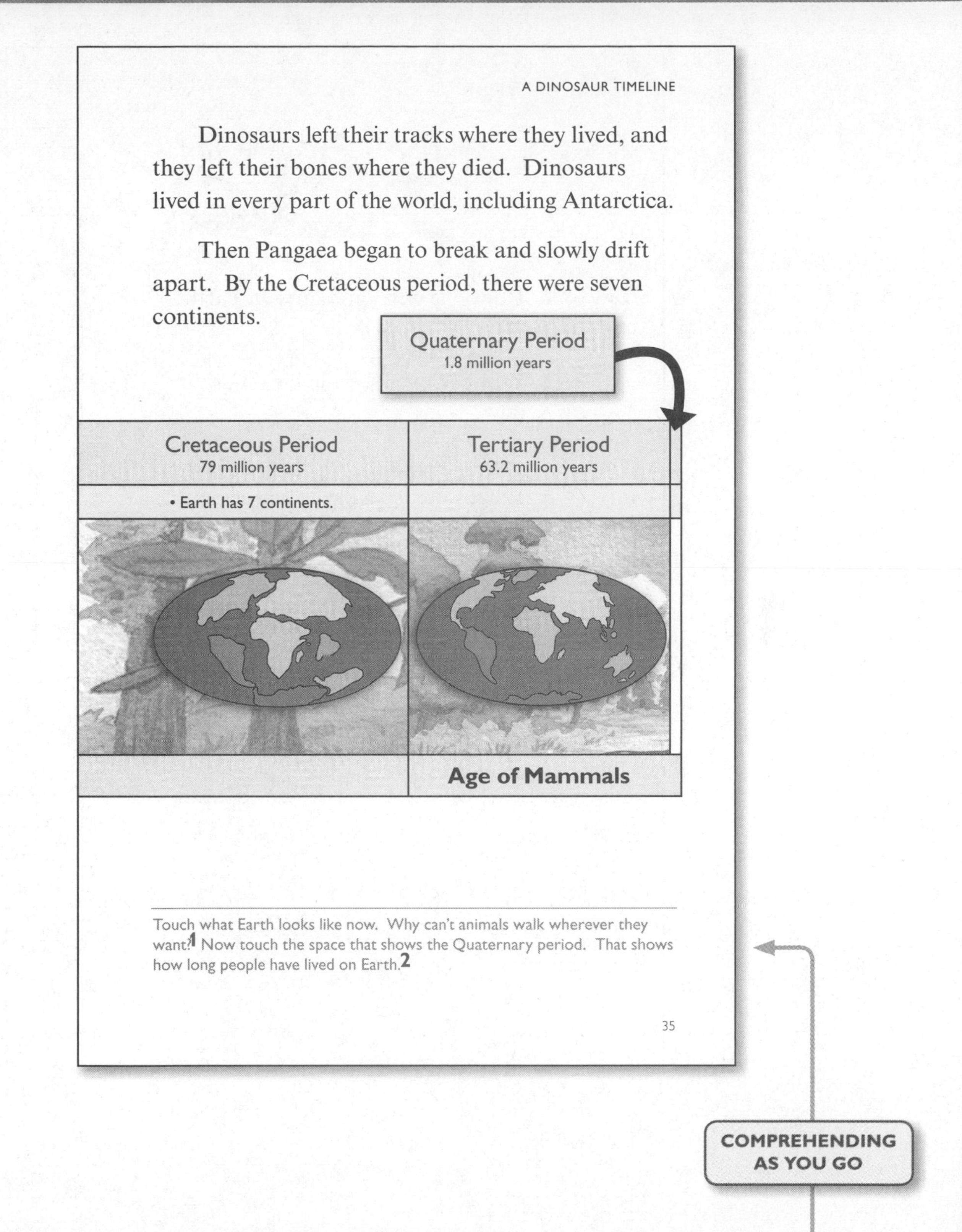

COMPREHENDING AS YOU GO

❶ **Understand:** Locating Information; **Apply:** Inferring, Explaining (Now there are seven continents, not one. There are oceans to cross so animals can't walk wherever they want.)

❷ **Understand:** Locating Information

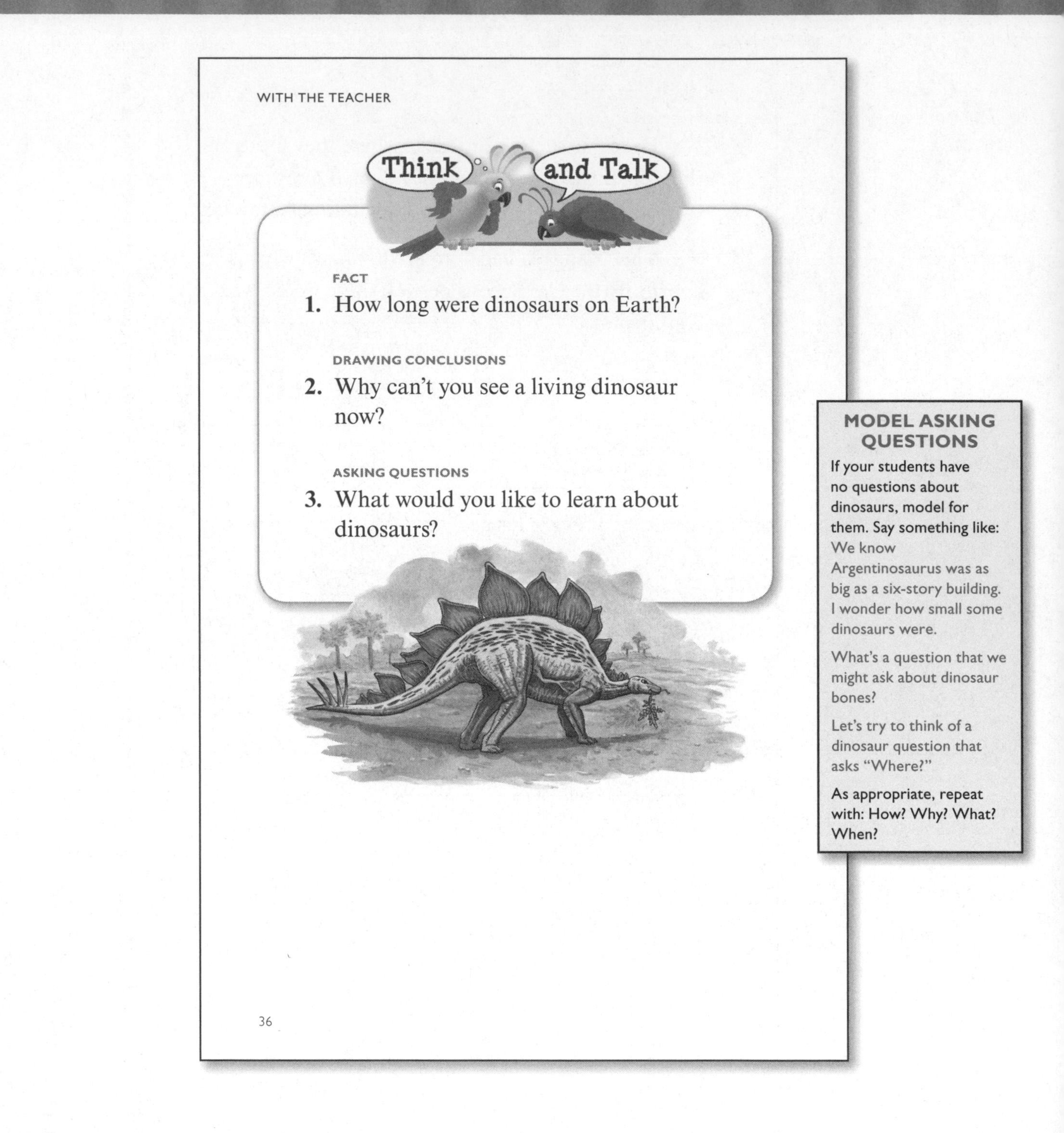

WITH THE TEACHER

Think and Talk

FACT

1. How long were dinosaurs on Earth?

DRAWING CONCLUSIONS

2. Why can't you see a living dinosaur now?

ASKING QUESTIONS

3. What would you like to learn about dinosaurs?

36

MODEL ASKING QUESTIONS

If your students have no questions about dinosaurs, model for them. Say something like: We know Argentinosaurus was as big as a six-story building. I wonder how small some dinosaurs were.

What's a question that we might ask about dinosaur bones?

Let's try to think of a dinosaur question that asks "Where?"

As appropriate, repeat with: How? Why? What? When?

❶ **Understand:** Explaining—Fact (Dinosaurs were on Earth for 165 million years.)

❷ **Analyze:** Drawing Conclusions; Using Vocabulary—extinct (Dinosaurs are extinct.)

❸ **Create:** Generating Ideas, Asking Questions (Why did they die? What did they eat . . .)

FACT SUMMARY

COMPREHENSION PROCESSES

Understand, Apply

WRITING TRAITS

Ideas and Content
Organization—Expository
Word Choice
Conventions—Complete Sentence, Capital, Period
Presentation

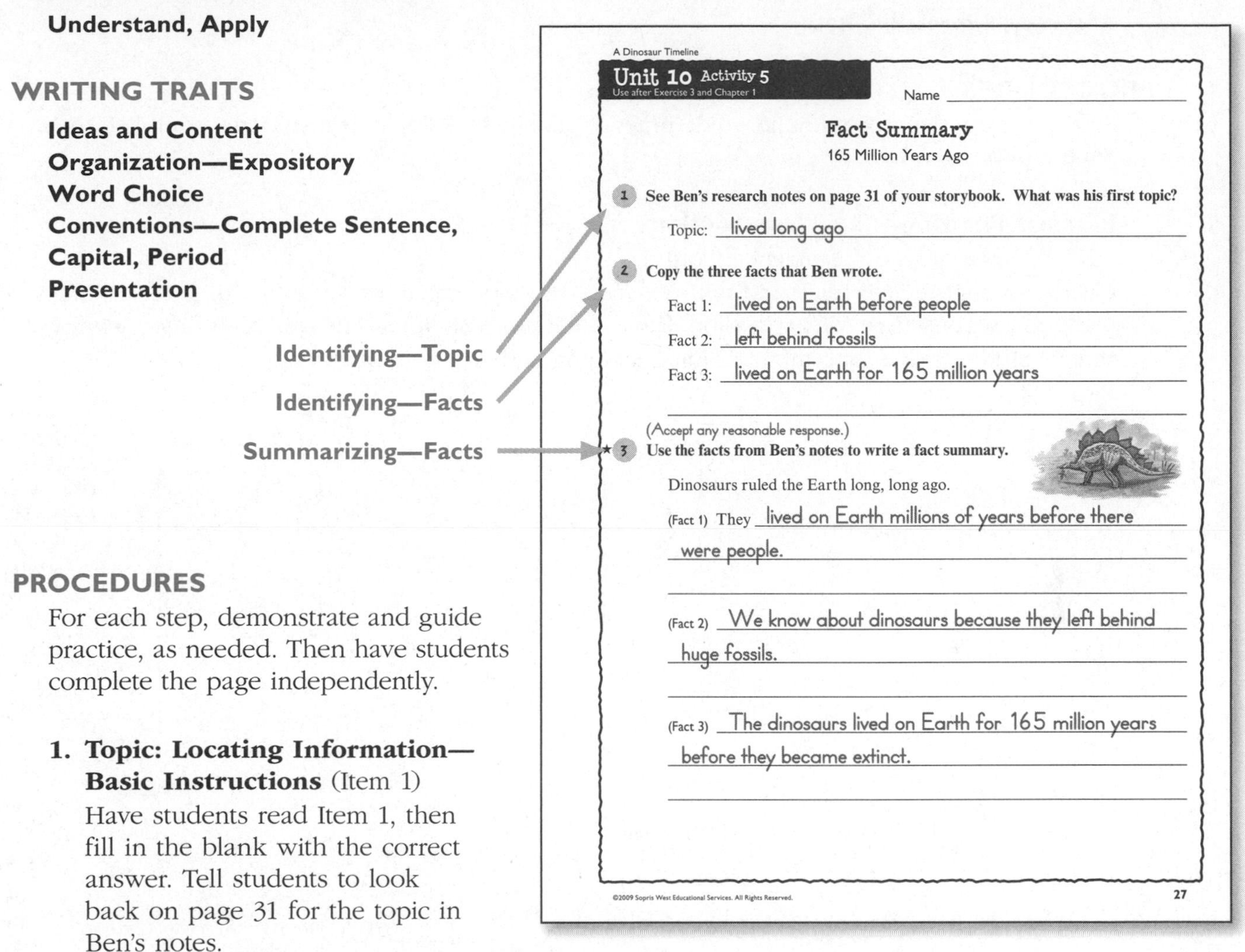

A Dinosaur Timeline

Unit 10 Activity 5
Use after Exercise 3 and Chapter 1

Name ____________

Fact Summary
165 Million Years Ago

1. See Ben's research notes on page 31 of your storybook. What was his first topic?
   Topic: lived long ago

2. Copy the three facts that Ben wrote.
   Fact 1: lived on Earth before people
   Fact 2: left behind fossils
   Fact 3: lived on Earth for 165 million years

(Accept any reasonable response.)

★ 3. Use the facts from Ben's notes to write a fact summary.

Dinosaurs ruled the Earth long, long ago.

(Fact 1) They lived on Earth millions of years before there were people.

(Fact 2) We know about dinosaurs because they left behind huge fossils.

(Fact 3) The dinosaurs lived on Earth for 165 million years before they became extinct.

 27

PROCEDURES

For each step, demonstrate and guide practice, as needed. Then have students complete the page independently.

1. **Topic: Locating Information—Basic Instructions** (Item 1)
   Have students read Item 1, then fill in the blank with the correct answer. Tell students to look back on page 31 for the topic in Ben's notes.

2. **Making Lists: Locating Information—Specific Instructions** (Item 2)
   - Have students copy the three facts from Ben's research notes. Say something like:
     Read the directions for Item 2. (Copy the three facts that Ben wrote.)
     You need to look in your storybook to find the facts that Ben wrote in his research notes.
     Turn to page 31. What should you copy next to the first fact? (lived on Earth before people)
   - Repeat, if needed, for Facts 2 and 3.

★ 3. **Fact Summary: Paragraph Writing—Specific Instructions** (Item 3)
   - Remind students that they practiced this activity in their Focus Lesson.
   - Have students read the topic sentence, then write their own fact summary by composing sentences about the three facts they listed in Item 2.
   - Encourage students to add details and snazzy words.
   - Remind students to start all sentences with a capital letter and end with a period.

Self-monitoring
Have students check and correct their work.

★ = New in this unit

PASSAGE READING FLUENCY

FLUENCY

Accuracy, Expression, Rate

PROCEDURES

For each step, demonstrate and guide practice, as needed. Then have students complete the page independently.

Passage Reading—Basic Instructions

- Have students read the practice words.
- Have students finger track and whisper read the story two times—the first time for accuracy and the second time for expression. Have students cross out a dinosaur each time they finish.
- Have students do a one-minute Timed Reading and cross out the timer.

ACCURACY PRECEDES RATE (Reminder)

Students should read the story with a high degree of accuracy before proceeding to Timed Readings. Reading for increased rate before establishing a high degree of accuracy may encourage students to guess at words.

A Dinosaur Timeline

Unit 10 Activity 6
Use after Exercise 3 and Chapter 1

Name ______________________

Passage Reading Fluency

1. Practice these words:

adventure	expedition	journey	squawked	ready

2. Read the story 2 times. Cross out a dinosaur each time you read the story.

Miss Tam Goes on a Dino Dig

Miss Tam sat at the kitchen table with a pile of books in front of her. Miss Tam said, "I'm ready for my next adventure." 15 25

Minnie Bird squawked, "Expedition." 29

Miss Tam said, "A special journey, an expedition? Why, Minnie Bird, that's a grand idea. Should I go on a moon expedition? An expedition under the sea? Or perhaps an expedition to the South Pole?" 39 52 64

A small paperback book dropped to the floor. Miss Tam picked it up and quickly read the first two chapters. "That's it!" she exclaimed. "I'll go on a dino dig, just like the Wright family." 76 88 99

3. Set a timer and see how far you can read in one minute.
Then cross out the timer.

28

CHECKOUT OPPORTUNITY

Listen to your students read individually while others work. When possible, provide your lowest-performing students with one-to-one practice.

❶ SOUND REVIEW

Have students read the sounds and key word phrases. Work for accuracy, then fluency.

❷ ACCURACY AND FLUENCY BUILDING

- For each task, have students say any underlined part, then read the word.
- Set a pace. Then have students read the whole words in each task and column.
- Provide repeated practice, building accuracy first, then fluency.

C1. Related Words

Tell students the related word. Then have them read the words.

All the words in this group are related to the word *cover.* Read the words.

D1. Word Endings

Have students read any underlined word, then the word with an ending.

Note: Tell students the y changes to i-e when you add s to "baby."

E1. Tricky Words

- For each Tricky Word, have students use the sounds and word parts they know to silently sound out the word. Use the word in a sentence to help with pronunciation.
- If the word is unfamiliar, tell students the word.

either

Look at the first word. The first part of this word is tricky. It's pronounced /ēēē/.

Say the word parts with me. ei-ther

I didn't want to go to the park and Edward didn't want to go . . . *either.*

Read the word three times. (either, either, either)

Eng•land

Look at the next word. Say the word parts with me. Eng • land

My great-grandfather is from . . . *England.* Read the word two times. (England, England)

given What's the best present you've ever been . . . *given?*

died When I forgot to feed my fish, they . . . *died.*

- Have students go back and read the whole words in the column.

❸ MULTISYLLABIC WORDS

For each word, have students read the syllables, then the whole word. Use the word in a sentence, as appropriate.

fossils Laura went on the expedition to look for . . . *fossils.*

possible Mack didn't think he could do it. He didn't think it was . . . *possible.*

fascinated Ben stared and stared at the dinosaur skeleton. He was . . . *fascinated.*

thighbone The upper bone in your leg is called the . . . *thighbone.*

❹ MORPHOGRAPHS AND AFFIXES

- Have students read the underlined part, then the word.
- Repeat practice with whole words, mixing group and individual turns.
  Build accuracy, then fluency.

❺ GENERALIZATION: READING NEW WORDS IN PARAGRAPHS

- Have students read the paragraph silently, then out loud. Tell students to use the sounds and word parts they know to read any difficult words.
- Repeat practice, as needed.

A Dinosaur Timeline

Unit 10 Exercise 4
Use before Chapter 2

1. SOUND REVIEW Have students review sounds for accuracy, then for fluency.

A	oo as in book	u as in umbrella	ph as in phone	ow as in snow	-dge as in badge
B	aw	ir	u_e	igh	ch

2. ACCURACY AND FLUENCY BUILDING For each column, have students say any underlined part, then read each word. Next, have students read the whole column.

A1 New Sound Practice	B1 Mixed Practice	C1 Related Words	D1 Word Endings	E1 Tricky Words
coast	laid	cover	formed	either
roach	wrong	covered	raised	England
coach	during	discover	turned	given
goal	never	discovered	guesses	died
	strange	discovering	finding	
	thigh		baby	
	found		babies	
	first			

3. MULTISYLLABIC WORDS Have students read each word part, then read each whole word.

A	fos•sils	fossils	pos•si•ble	possible
B	fas•ci•nat•ed	fascinated	thigh•bone	thighbone

4. MORPHOGRAPHS AND AFFIXES Have students read the underlined word part, then the word.

lovely	remains	cheerful	excited

5. GENERALIZATION Have students read the paragraph silently, then out loud. (New words: dragon, lizard)

My brother's birthday is tomorrow. I dashed to the store with Mom because I realized that I forgot to get him a present. There were so many cool things at the store. I saw a giant dinosaur, an enormous dragon, and a terrible-looking lizard. Mom said to get either the dinosaur or the dragon. My guess is my brother would love any of these things!

21

TEACHER SELF-MONITORING (Reminder)

- Are you gently correcting all errors?
- Are you returning to difficult words for three correct responses?
- Are you mixing group and individual turns?
- Are you repeating practice until students are accurate and fluent?
- Are you preteaching the lowest performers in your group?

(See *Getting Started* to understand why these strategies are critical to student success.)

CHAPTER 2 INSTRUCTIONS

Students read Chapter 2 with the teacher.

COMPREHENSION PROCESSES

Understand, Apply, Analyze, Create, Evaluate

PROCEDURES

1. Reviewing Chapter 1

Summarizing—Facts

Say something like:

In Chapter 1, Ben showed us how to write research notes.

His first topic was "Dinosaurs Lived Long Ago." What facts did he write? (lived on Earth long before people . . .)

RESEARCH NOTES
Topic 1: Dinosaurs Lived Long Ago
Fact 1: lived on Earth long before people
Fact 2: left behind fossils
Fact 3: lived on Earth for 165 million years

PREP NOTE

Copy the research notes on a board or chart before calling your group.

2. Introducing and Setting the Purpose for Chapter 2

Identifying—Title

Have students identify the title. Explain that you will be adding to the research notes.

Say something like:

What's the title of this chapter? (Discovering Dinosaurs)

We're going to add to Ben's research notes in this chapter.

3. First Reading

- Ask questions and discuss the story as indicated by the gray text.
- Mix group and individual turns, independent of your voice.
  Have students work toward a group accuracy goal of 0–4 errors.
- After reading the story, practice any difficult words.

4. Partner or Whisper Reading: Repeated Reading

Before beginning independent work, have students finger track and partner or whisper read.

5. Comprehension and Skill Work

Tell students they will do Comprehension and Skill Activities 7 and 8 after they read Chapter 2. Guide practice, as needed. (For teacher directions, see pages 77 and 78.)

6. Homework 4: Repeated Reading

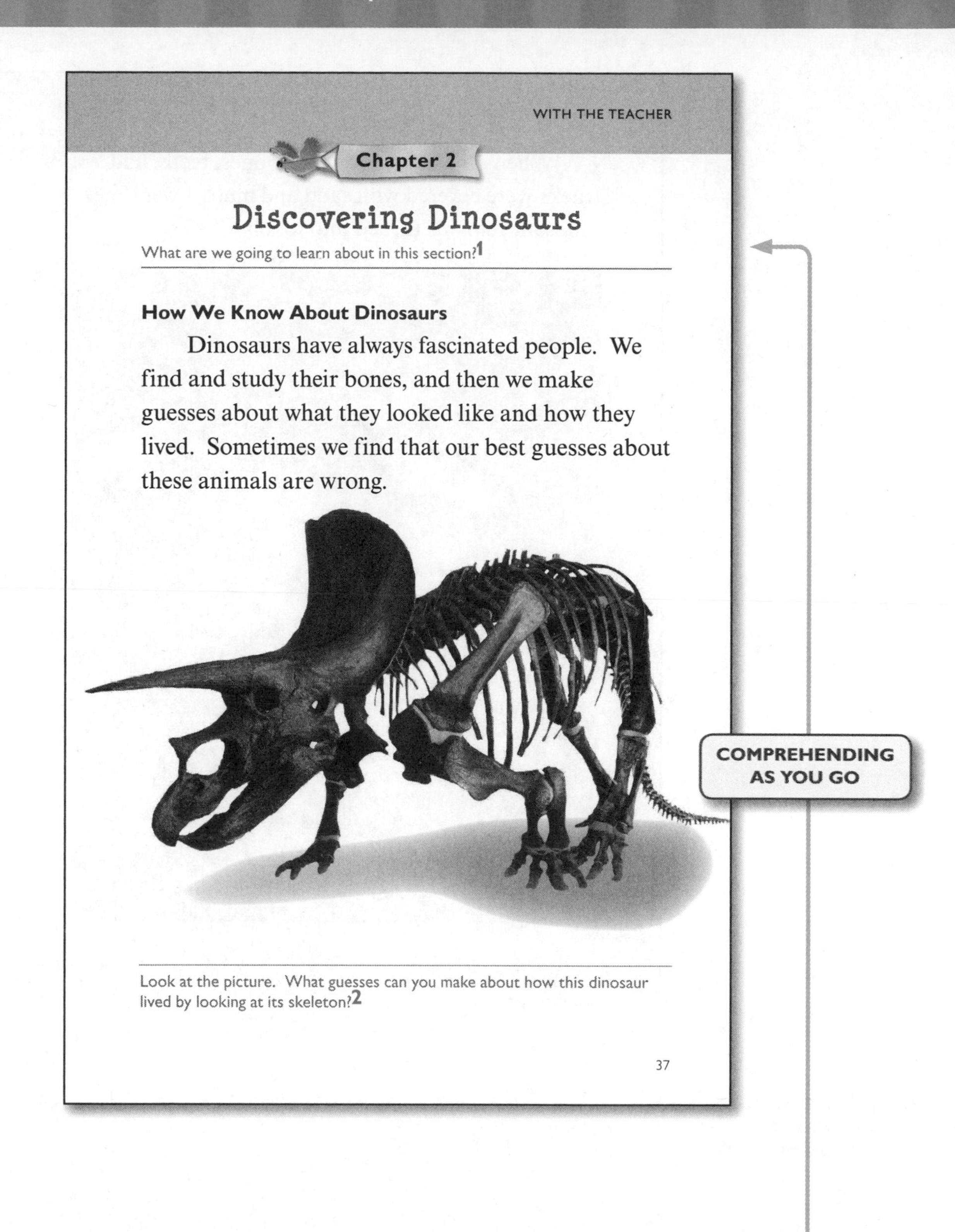

WITH THE TEACHER

Chapter 2

Discovering Dinosaurs

What are we going to learn about in this section?[1]

How We Know About Dinosaurs

Dinosaurs have always fascinated people. We find and study their bones, and then we make guesses about what they looked like and how they lived. Sometimes we find that our best guesses about these animals are wrong.

Look at the picture. What guesses can you make about how this dinosaur lived by looking at its skeleton?[2]

37

COMPREHENDING AS YOU GO

❶ **Understand:** Using Headings; **Apply:** Inferring—Topic (We will learn about how people discovered dinosaurs.)

❷ **Analyze:** Viewing, Inferring; **Apply:** Using Vocabulary—protect (It has a big horn, so it probably needed to protect itself. Its head is near the ground, so it probably ate plants . . .)

WITH THE TEACHER

When dinosaurs died, their bones, teeth, and tracks were covered with sand and mud. Over time, dinosaur remains turned into fossils.

Look at the picture. If you were on this dino dig, what would you be thinking?[1]

38

COMPREHENDING AS YOU GO

1 **Understand:** Viewing, Making Connections; **Evaluate:** Responding (I would be thinking about what kind of dinosaur it was, how much work there would be to dig it out . . .)

Fossils

TOPIC 2: FOSSILS
Fact 1:

What are we going to learn about in this section?[1] I'll write the topic in our research notes. As we read, listen for facts that explain how fossils are formed.

How is it possible to find the remains of dinosaurs millions of years after they died out? This is what happened.

Like other animals, dinosaurs lived, laid eggs, raised babies, and then died. If a dinosaur died near a stream, the sand and mud from the stream covered up the body. Over time, the dinosaur remains turned into stone and became fossils. Today, we find dinosaur fossils all over the world.

TOPIC 2: FOSSILS
Fact 1: Dino died
Fact 2:
Fact 3:

Find two or three facts that I can write in our notes that explain how *fossils* are formed. Look in your book for what happens first. What happens next?[2]

CONTINUE WITH RESEARCH NOTES

This process provides explicit instruction on how to take research notes.

As you guide students through the gray text, add to the notes on a chart or chalkboard.

COMPREHENDING AS YOU GO

RESEARCH NOTES (*continued*)

Topic 2: How were fossils formed?

Fact 1: A dino died.

Fact 2: Sand and mud covered up the dino.

Fact 3: The bones turned to stone.

❶ **Apply:** Inferring—Topic (We will learn how fossils are formed.)

❷ **Understand:** Locating Information; Summarizing—Facts; Using Vocabulary—dinosaur, remains, fossils (First, a dinosaur dies near a stream. Next, sand and mud cover the dinosaur's body. Then the remains turn into stone and become fossils.)

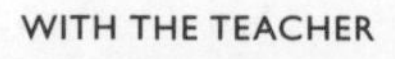

WITH THE TEACHER

Finding Fossils Long Ago

What are we going to learn about in this section? 1
What's the next topic to write on our research notes? 2

Listen for two or three facts that tell what people thought about dinosaurs long ago.

For thousands of years, people have been finding dinosaur fossils. One of the first dinosaur fossils was found in China more than 3,500 years ago. Imagine finding a large, strange-looking tooth. The people in China didn't know about dinosaurs, so they thought they had discovered the tooth of a dragon!

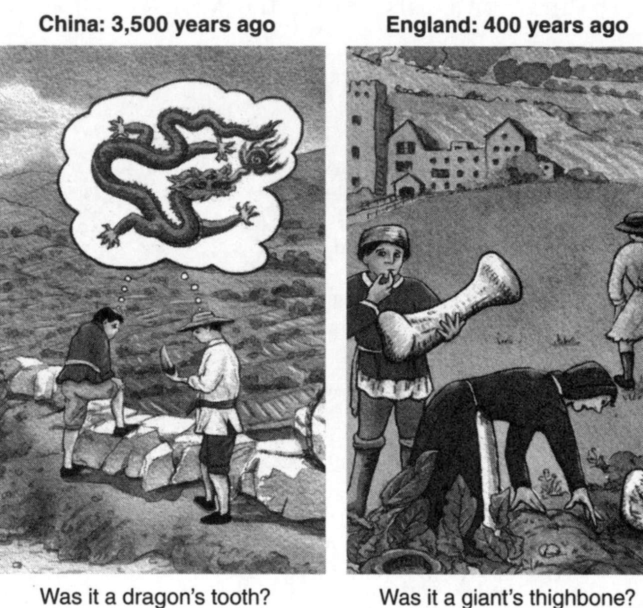

Was it a dragon's tooth? Was it a giant's thighbone?

40

COMPREHENDING AS YOU GO

RESEARCH NOTES
(continued)
Topic 3: Finding Fossils Long Ago

❶ **Apply:** Inferring—Topic (We will learn how people long ago found fossils.)
❷ **Understand:** Explaining—Topic (The next topic is finding fossils long ago.)

About 400 years ago in England, people found an enormous thighbone. The people of England didn't know about dinosaurs either. They thought they had found the bone of a giant!

During the next few hundred years, more and more bones were discovered. Finally, about 150 years ago, people realized the bones were from animals they had never seen. The animals were given the name dinosaur, which means terrible lizard.

TOPIC 3: FINDING FOSSILS

Fact 1: China, 3500 years Dragon's Tooth

What facts can we write in our notes? What did people think about dinosaurs 3,500 years ago, 400 years ago, and 150 years ago?[1]

RESEARCH NOTES (*continued*)

Topic 3: Finding Fossils Long Ago

Fact 1: 3,500 years ago, thought bones were from dragons

Fact 2: 400 years ago, thought bones were from giants

Fact 3: 150 years ago, thought bones were from dinosaurs

COMPREHENDING AS YOU GO

1 **Understand:** Summarizing—Facts (People who found a dinosaur tooth 3,500 years ago thought it came from a dragon. People who found a bone 400 years ago thought it came from a giant. People realized about 150 years ago that the bones came from animals they had never seen.)

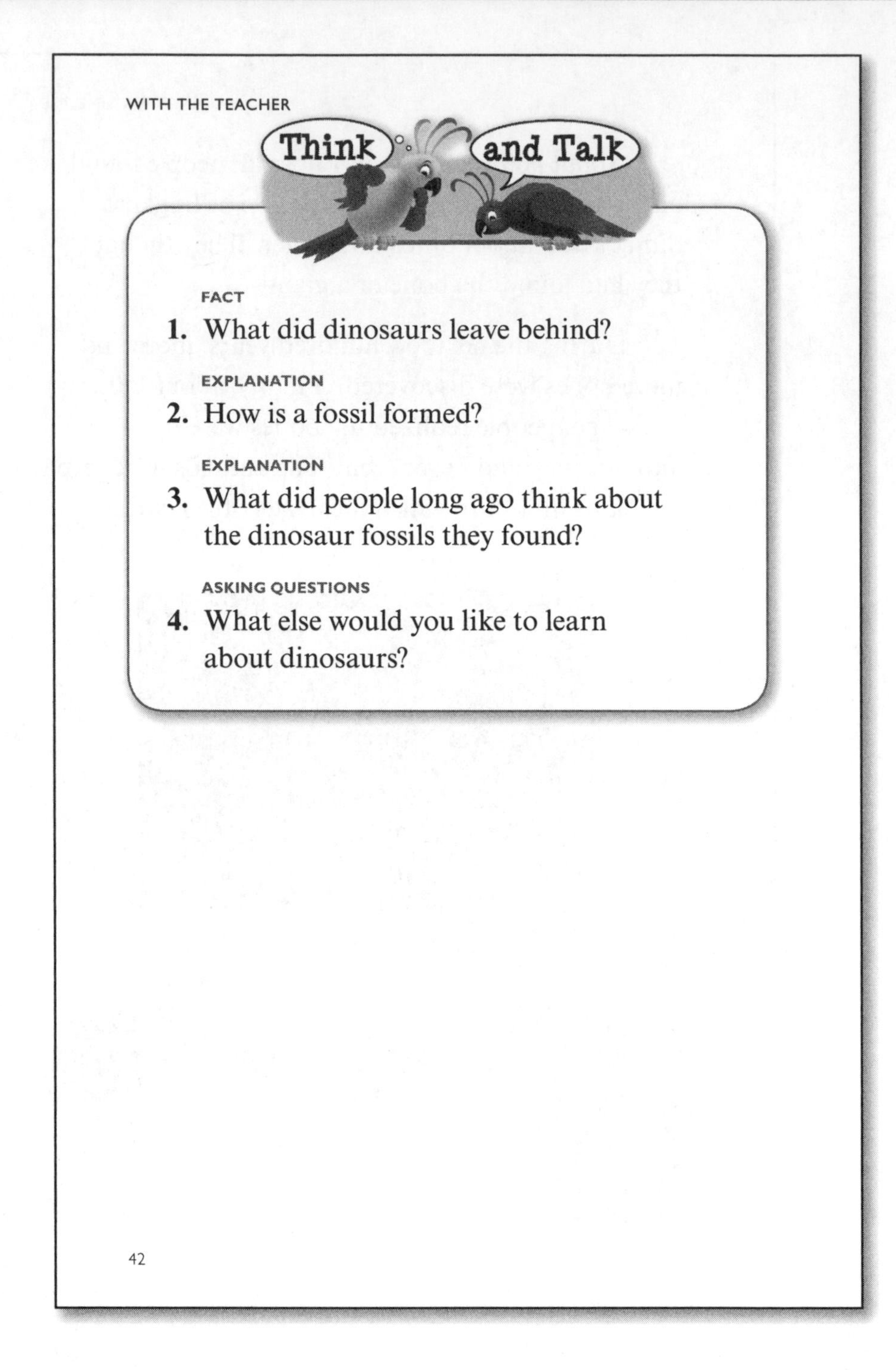

1 **Understand:** Explaining—Fact; Using Vocabulary—remains (They left their remains.)

2 **Understand:** Explaining—Facts (First, a dinosaur dies near a stream. Then sand and mud cover the dinosaur's body. Then the remains turn into stone and become fossils.)

3 **Understand:** Explaining—Facts (People who found a dinosaur tooth 3,500 years ago thought it came from a dragon. People who found a bone 400 years ago thought it came from a giant. People realized about 150 years ago that the bones came from animals they had never seen.)

4 **Create:** Generating Ideas, Asking Questions (How many dinosaurs have people found? Did any dinosaurs have feathers? Could dinosaurs swim . . .)

PASSAGE COMPREHENSION

COMPREHENSION PROCESSES

Understand, Apply

Identifying—Headings, Topics

Identifying—Facts; Test Taking

Using Graphic Organizer
Comparing/Contrasting

A Dinosaur Timeline

Unit 10 Activity 7
Use after Exercise 4 and Chapter 2

Name ______

Passage Comprehension

Discovering Dinosaurs

Look at the headings in your storybook.

1 **List the topics you read about in Chapter 2, Discovering Dinosaurs.**
(Accept any reasonable response.)
- how we know about dinosaurs
- how fossils are formed
- finding fossils long ago

★ 2 **Dinosaur Facts: Read the sentences and check the box for "Yes" or "No."**

	Yes, it is true.	No, it is not true.
We know about dinosaurs from their bones.	☑	☐
Dinosaur fossils are found all over the world.	☑	☐
The word *dinosaur* means fat dog.	☐	☑
The word *dinosaur* means terrible lizard.	☑	☐

3 **Across time, what did people think when they found dinosaur fossils?**
Complete the chart.

	China • 3,500 years ago	England • 400 years ago
What did people find?	huge tooth	enormous thighbone
What did people think the fossil was?	tooth of a dragon	bone of a giant

 29

PROCEDURES

For each step, demonstrate and guide practice, as needed.

1. **Topics: Locating Information—Specific Instructions** (Item 1)
   Have students read the directions and look in their storybooks for the topics/headings in Chapter 2. Have students write the topics.

★ 2. **True/False: Selection Response** (Item 2)

3. **Compare/Contrast: Matrix—Specific Instructions** (Item 3)
   - Have students read the question.
   - Review what a matrix is and its purpose. Say something like:
     A matrix is a chart that organizes information so you can see how things are the same and how they are different.
     What does a matrix show? (It shows how things are the same and how they are different.)
   - Have students read the headings for each column and identify what it tells about.
   - Have students compare information for Row 1.
     Read the question in the first row. (What did people find?)
     Now look at the headings. The first column will show what people in China found 3,500 years ago. What will the second column show? (what people in England found 400 years ago)
     What did people in China find? (a huge tooth) That's what you'll write in the box.

     What did they find in England? (an enormous thighbone)
     Let's look at the whole row. People in China found a huge tooth. People in England found a huge thighbone. The huge tooth and huge thighbone were . . . dinosaur fossils.
     Long ago in ancient China and old England, people found dinosaur fossils.
     Do you think they knew what they had found?
   - Repeat with Row 2. Discuss what was the same and what was different about what the people in China and England thought the dinosaur fossils were.

★ = New in this unit

PASSAGE COMPREHENSION • SEQUENCE OF EVENTS

COMPREHENSION PROCESSES

Understand, Apply

WRITING TRAITS

Organization—Expository
Conventions—Period
Presentation

PROCEDURES

For each step, demonstrate and guide practice, as needed. Then have students complete the page independently.

1. **Sequence of Events: Chart—Basic Instructions** (Item 1)
   - Have students read the directions and sentence starters, then fill in the blanks to complete the events.
   - Think aloud with students and discuss possible answers, as needed.

★ 2. **Sequence of Events: Paragraph Writing—Basic Instructions** (Item 2)
Have students read the instructions and write a paragraph using the events from the graphic organizer. Remind them to end sentences with a period.

Self-monitoring
Have students check and correct their work.

★ = New in this unit

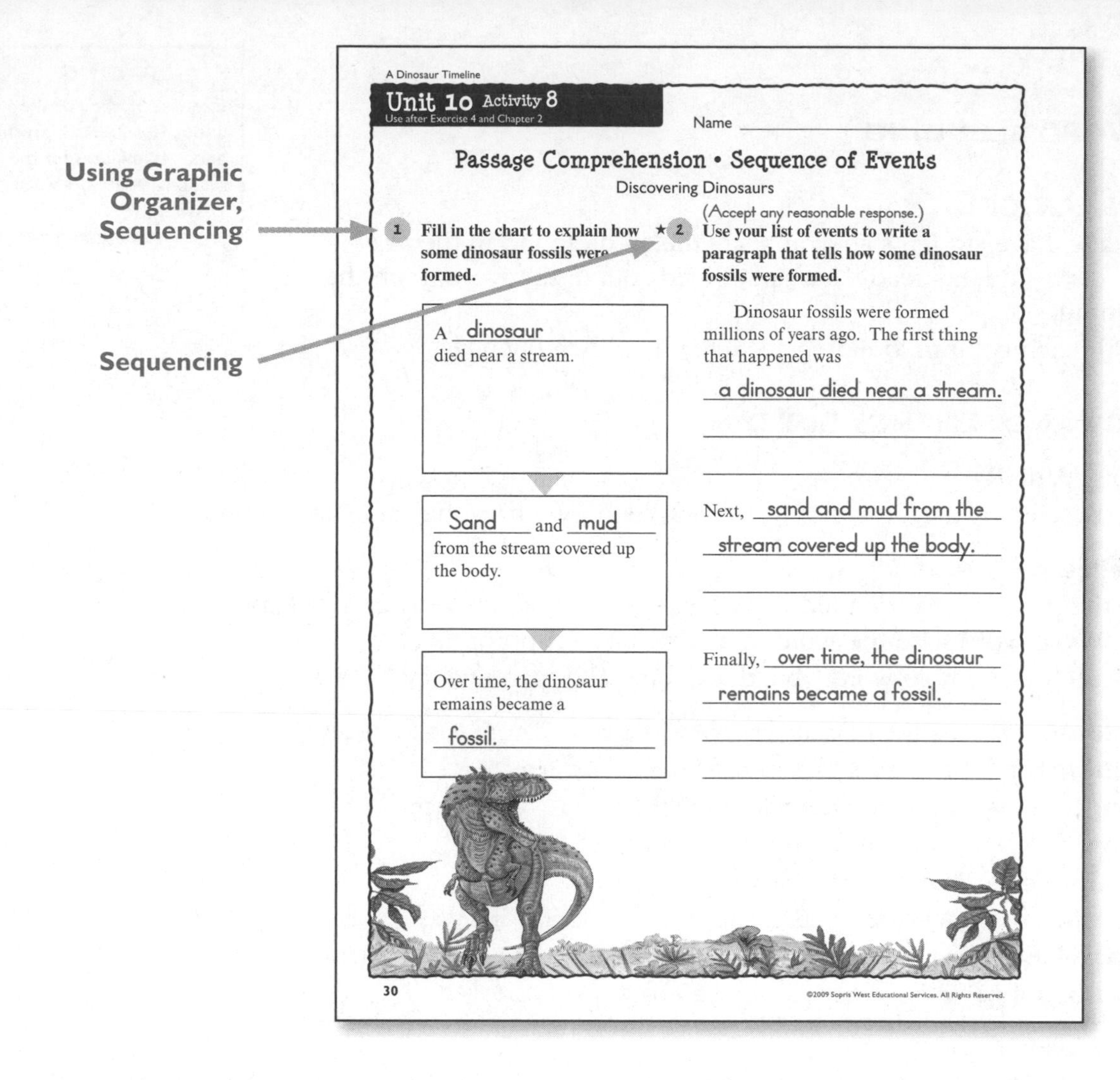

Using Graphic Organizer, Sequencing

Sequencing

A Dinosaur Timeline

Unit 10 Activity 8
Use after Exercise 4 and Chapter 2

Name ______________________

Passage Comprehension • Sequence of Events

Discovering Dinosaurs

(Accept any reasonable response.)

1 **Fill in the chart to explain how some dinosaur fossils were formed.**

A dinosaur died near a stream.

Sand and mud from the stream covered up the body.

Over time, the dinosaur remains became a fossil.

★ **2** **Use your list of events to write a paragraph that tells how some dinosaur fossils were formed.**

Dinosaur fossils were formed millions of years ago. The first thing that happened was a dinosaur died near a stream.

Next, sand and mud from the stream covered up the body.

Finally, over time, the dinosaur remains became a fossil.

30

❶ SOUND REVIEW

> **PACING**
> Exercise 5a should take about 10 minutes, allowing about 10 minutes for the Fictional Narrative Focus Lesson.

❷ SHIFTY WORD BLENDING

❸ SOUND PRACTICE

- For each task, have students spell and say the focus sound in the gray bar. Next, have students read each underlined sound, the word, then the whole column.
- Repeat with each column, building accuracy first, then fluency.

❹ ACCURACY AND FLUENCY BUILDING

B1. Rhyming Words

Have students read each set of words and identify what's the same about them.

C1. Multisyllabic Words

- For the list of words divided by syllables, have students read each syllable, then read the whole word. Use the word in a sentence, as appropriate.
- For the list of whole words, build accuracy and then fluency.

skeleton At the museum, there was a large dinosaur . . . *skeleton.*
excitement The dogs barked at all the . . . *excitement.*
complete Finally, Sean's science project was . . . *complete.*
plaster Paolo made a funny mask out of . . . *plaster.*
continued Next week, the story will be . . . *continued.*
obsessed All Amanda thought about was dolls. She was . . . *obsessed.*
dynamite They blasted through the mountain with . . . *dynamite.*
paintbrushes We painted the house with . . . *paintbrushes.*

D1. Tricky Words

- For each Tricky Word, have students use the sounds and word parts they know to silently sound out the word. Use the word in a sentence to help with pronunciation.
- If the word is unfamiliar, tell students the word.

wars
Look at the first word. The word is *wars.* Say the word. (wars)
Fights between countries are called . . . *wars.*
Read the word three times. (wars, wars, wars)

shovels
Look at the next word. Say the word parts with me. shov-els
The workers dug the holes with . . . *shovels.* Read the word two times. (shovels, shovels)

special Grandma thinks I am very . . . *special.*

D2. Story Words

Tell students the underlined sound, then have them read the word.

❺ MORPHOGRAPHS AND AFFIXES

❻ NAMES AND PLACES

Have students use the sounds and word parts they know to figure out the words.

7 DINOSAUR WORDS

Have students read the word, using the pronunciation guide for help.

A Dinosaur Timeline

Unit 10 Exercise 5a

Use before Chapter 3

1. SOUND REVIEW Use selected Sound Cards from Units 1–10.

2. SHIFTY WORD BLENDING For each word, have students say the underlined part, sound out smoothly, then read the word.

bone	phone	stone	stole	steal

3. SOUND PRACTICE In each column, have students spell and say the sound, then say any underlined sound and the word. Next, have students read the whole column.

oa	ue, ew	ci, ce	Mixed Practice
coat	glue	places	number
roam	Sue	excite	notes
boast	knew	fascinate	picks
toast	grew	fascinating	rush

4. ACCURACY AND FLUENCY BUILDING For each column, have students say any underlined part, then read each word. Next, have students read the whole column.

A1 Word Endings	B1 Rhyming Words	C1 Multisyllabic Words		D1 Tricky Words
hunters	cried	skel•e•ton	skeleton	wars
stolen	tried	ex•cite•ment	excitement	shovels
fossils	spied	com•plete	complete	special
bickered		plas•ter	plaster	**D2 Story Words**
shipped	pictures	con•tin•ued	continued	imagine
chipped	adventures	ob•sessed	obsessed	curious
	creatures	dy•na•mite	dynamite	destroyed
		paint•brush•es	paintbrushes	

5. MORPHOGRAPHS AND AFFIXES Have students read the underlined word part, then the word.

A	untouched	rebuild	research	nearly
B	carefully	finally	determined	comfortable

6. NAMES AND PLACES Have students use the sounds and word parts they know to figure out the words.

Edward Cope	Charles Marsh	New Jersey	United States

7. DINOSAUR WORDS Have students use the sounds and word parts they know and the pronunciation guide to read the word.

Hadrosaurus	Had-roh-sore-us

22

ENCOURAGING DESIRED BEHAVIORS

Make a special effort to notice and congratulate the least mature students whenever they are taking steps toward greater cooperation, responsibility, and independence.

★FICTION, NARRATIVE

FOCUS LESSON
Skills and Strategies

PURPOSE

The purpose of this lesson is to provide explicit instruction in how to use a story frame to complete a narrative. The lesson prepares students for Comprehension and Skill Work. Students do not write in their books.

PREP NOTES

To demonstrate how to write a narrative, use an overhead of page 23 in student *Exercise Book 2,* write on a transparency placed over the page, or use a paper copy.

PACING

This part of your lesson should take about 10 minutes.

COMPREHENSION PROCESSES

Create

PROCEDURES

1 INTRODUCTION

Identifying—Genre

Explain the purpose of the lesson. Say something like:
"Going on a Dino Dig" is a fictional story about a dinosaur expedition.
It is a made-up story, so it's called . . . fiction.
Today, we're going to write a shared story about going on a dino dig. Then in Comp and Skill Work, you will write your own Dino Dig story.

2 BRAINSTORMING, WRITING THE STORY INTRODUCTION

Generating Ideas—Initiating Event

Have students read the frame for the introduction, then brainstorm possible initiating events. Say something like: Our story, or narrative, is going to begin with "When I was blank years old, the most amazing thing happened." Let's use *eight* for the blank. **Write "eight" in the blank.**
Next, we need to figure out how to get on a dino dig. One exciting idea is already written for us. Our story could start, "I won a raffle and got to go on a dino dig." Wouldn't that be fun! What are some other ways that you might get to go on a dino dig? (Maybe I could get an invitation. . . .)
Remember those ideas. They would all make great starts for your own dino dig story.

3 WRITING THE BODY OF THE FICTIONAL NARRATIVE

Generating Ideas—Action, Conclusion; Word Choice

- Using the story frame, guide how to write the body of your fictional narrative.
  Say something like: Read the beginning of the next paragraph. (The dino expedition was . . .)
  Partner 1, tell your partner a snazzy word for what the dino expedition was like.
  Wait about 20 seconds, give Partner 2 time to brainstorm snazzy words, then have the group share possibilities. Write one word in the blank.
- Have students read the next sentence.
  Read the next part of our story. (First, we were given shovels, picks, and brushes.)
  What do you think would happen next on a dino dig?
- Guide students as they generate ideas for the next two parts of the story.
  What do you think would happen next on a dino dig?
  After "Next," write "we dug and dug. Phew! It was hard work."
  Now, let's think of something fun and exciting for the final part of the story.
  After "Finally," write "We found dinosaur bones. We were excited."
- Have students read the first paragraphs then guide writing the conclusion.

★= New in this unit

❹ USING THE CHECK AND CORRECT BOX

Demonstrate how to use the Check and Correct box to fix errors.

A Dinosaur Timeline

Unit 10 Exercise 5b (Focus Lesson)

Use after Exercise 5a and before Chapter 3

FOCUS LESSON Skills and Strategies

★Fiction, Narrative My Story

STOP Don't write in your Exercise Book.

Going on a Dino Dig

When I was eight years old, the most amazing thing happened. I won a raffle and got to go on a dino dig.

The dino expedition was exciting.

First, we were given shovels, picks, and brushes.

Next, we dug and dug. Phew! It was hard work.

Finally, we found dinosaur bones. We were excited.

I wish I could go on another dig. It was the best!

✓ Check and Correct

1. Do your sentences make sense? ☑
2. Do the sentences tell the story? ☑
3. Do you have a capital at the beginning of each sentence and a period at the end? ☑
4. Did you use your best handwriting? ☑

 Blackline Master 23

COMPREHENSION PROCESSES

Understand, Apply

PROCEDURES

★obsessed ★boast ★bicker, dinosaur, curious

1. **Introducing Vocabulary**
   - For each vocabulary word, have students read the word by parts, then read the whole word.
   - Read the student-friendly explanations to students as they follow with their fingers. Then have students use the vocabulary word by following the gray text.
   - Review and discuss the photos and illustrations.

2. **Now You Try It!**
   - Read or paraphrase the directions.
   - For each word, have students read the word by parts, then read the whole word.
   - Have students explain or define each word in their own words.
     Say something like:
     Look at the word. Read the whole word. (dinosaur)
     Now let's pretend that we're going to explain or define the word *dinosaur* to a friend. [Jasmin], what would you say? Start with "A *dinosaur* is . . . " (A dinosaur is an animal that lived long ago.)
     Very good. What else might we say about a dinosaur?
   - Have students turn to the appropriate page in the glossary and discuss how their definitions are the same as or different from the glossary's.

★= New in this unit

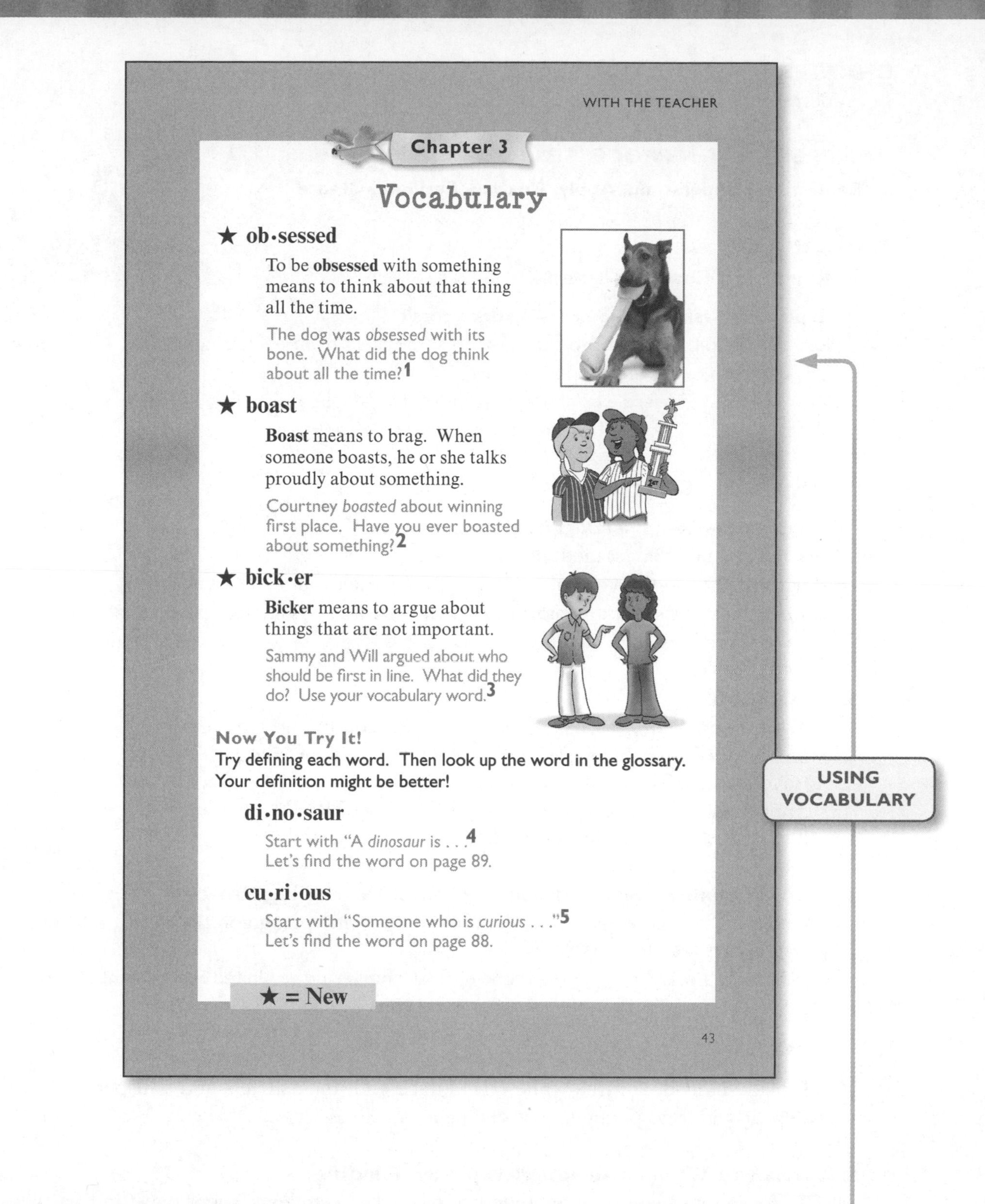

WITH THE TEACHER

Chapter 3

Vocabulary

★ **ob•sessed**

To be **obsessed** with something means to think about that thing all the time.

The dog was *obsessed* with its bone. What did the dog think about all the time?1

★ **boast**

Boast means to brag. When someone boasts, he or she talks proudly about something.

Courtney *boasted* about winning first place. Have you ever boasted about something?2

★ **bick•er**

Bicker means to argue about things that are not important.

Sammy and Will argued about who should be first in line. What did they do? Use your vocabulary word.3

Now You Try It!

Try defining each word. Then look up the word in the glossary. Your definition might be better!

di•no•saur

Start with "A *dinosaur* is . . ."4
Let's find the word on page 89.

cu•ri•ous

Start with "Someone who is *curious* . . ."5
Let's find the word on page 88.

★ = New

43

USING VOCABULARY

❶ **Understand:** Defining Vocabulary—obsessed (The dog thought about the bone all the time.)

❷ **Apply:** Using Vocabulary—boast (I boasted when my drawing won first prize in the contest.)

❸ **Understand:** Using Vocabulary—bicker (Sammy and Will bickered about who should be first in line.)

❹ **Understand:** Defining and Using Vocabulary—dinosaur; Using Glossary (A dinosaur is an extinct animal that roamed Earth millions of years ago.)

❺ **Understand:** Defining and Using Vocabulary—curious; Using Glossary (Someone who is curious wants to know more about something.)

CHAPTER 3 INSTRUCTIONS

Students read Chapter 3 with the teacher.

COMPREHENSION PROCESSES

Remember, Understand, Apply, Analyze, Evaluate, Create

PROCEDURES

1. Reviewing Chapters 1 and 2

Explaining; Using Vocabulary—extinct, fossil

Review Chapters 1 and 2 by discussing some facts from each chapter. Say something like:

Has a person ever seen a dinosaur? (no)

Why not? (They were extinct before there were people on Earth.)

What is a fossil? (A fossil is a bone that turned into rock over a long time.)

2. Introducing Chapter 3

Identifying—Title; Inferring; Predicting

Discuss the title. Say something like:

What's the title of this chapter? (Hunting for Dinosaurs in the United States)

Do you think there were dinosaurs in the United States? What makes you think so?

(The Wrights went on a dino dig. The story said that dinosaurs lived all over the world.)

3. First Reading

- Ask questions and discuss the story as indicated by the gray text.
- Mix group and individual turns, independent of your voice. Have students work toward a group accuracy goal of 0–5 errors.
- After reading the story, practice any difficult words. Repeat if students have not reached the accuracy goal.

CORRECTING DECODING ERRORS

During story reading, gently correct any error, then have students reread the sentence.

4. Second Reading, Short Passage Practice: Developing Prosody

- Demonstrate expressive, fluent reading on the first paragraph. Read at a rate slightly faster than the students' rate.

  "About 150 years ago, people found dinosaur bones in the United States. A nearly . . . "

- Guide practice with your voice.

  Read the first paragraph with me. About 150 years ago . . .

- Provide individual turns while others track with their fingers and whisper read.
- Repeat with one paragraph or one page at a time.

5. Partner or Whisper Reading: Repeated Reading

Before beginning independent work, have students finger track and partner or whisper read.

6. Comprehension and Skill Work

Tell students they will do Comprehension and Skill Activities 9 and 10 after they read Chapter 3. Guide practice, as needed. (For teacher directions, see pages 94 and 95.)

7. Homework 5: Repeated Reading

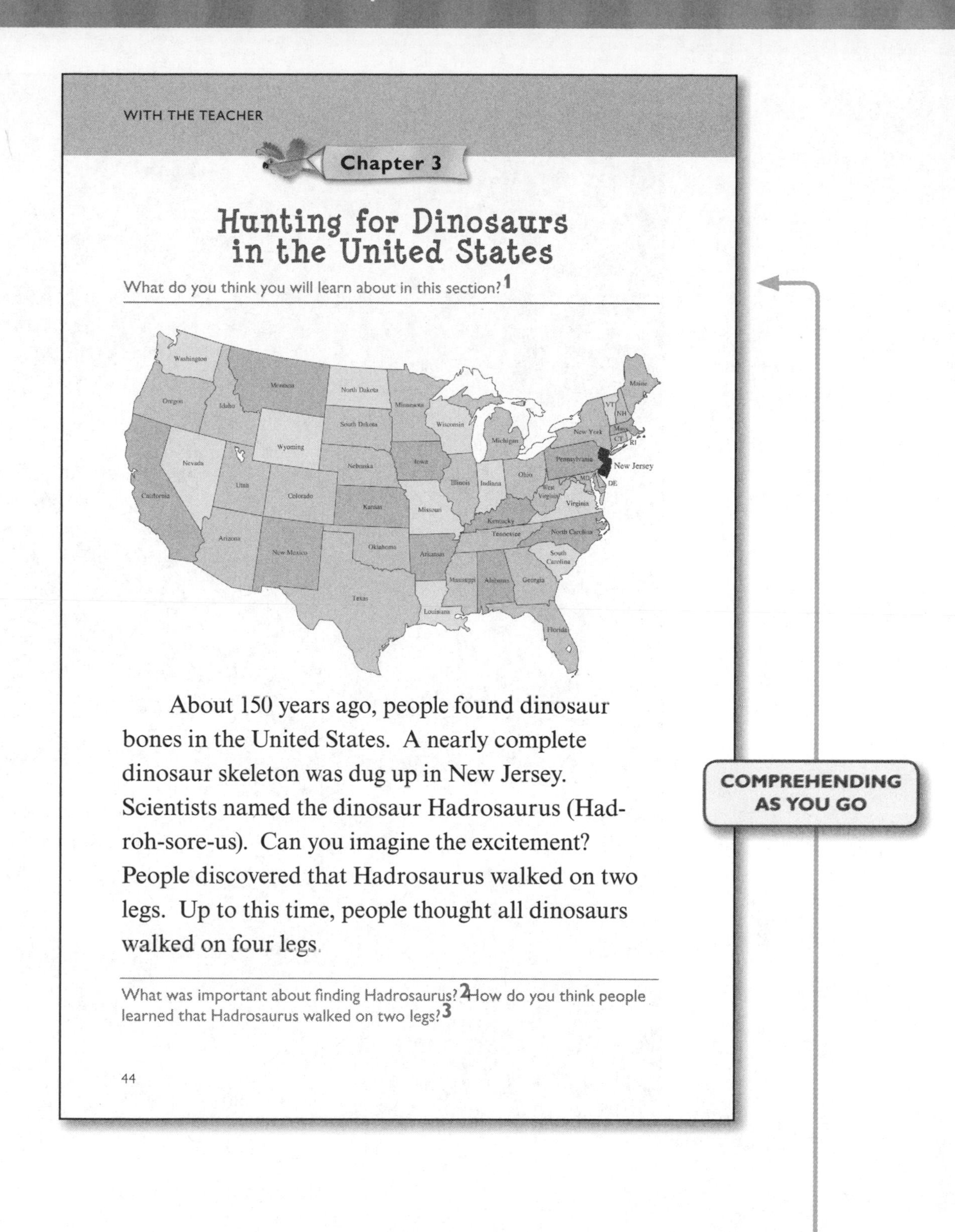

WITH THE TEACHER

Chapter 3

Hunting for Dinosaurs in the United States

What do you think you will learn about in this section?[1]

About 150 years ago, people found dinosaur bones in the United States. A nearly complete dinosaur skeleton was dug up in New Jersey. Scientists named the dinosaur Hadrosaurus (Had-roh-sore-us). Can you imagine the excitement? People discovered that Hadrosaurus walked on two legs. Up to this time, people thought all dinosaurs walked on four legs.

What was important about finding Hadrosaurus?[2] How do you think people learned that Hadrosaurus walked on two legs?[3]

44

COMPREHENDING AS YOU GO

❶ **Apply:** Inferring—Topic (We will learn about how people hunted for dinosaurs in the United States.)

❷ **Apply:** Inferring, Explaining (It was the first dinosaur found in the United States. It was the first dinosaur found that had walked on two legs.)

❷ **Apply:** Inferring (I think they put a Hadrosaurus skeleton together and realized that the front legs were much shorter than the back legs.)

A DINOSAUR TIMELINE
45

WITH THE TEACHER

The Bone Wars

What are you going to learn about in this section?[1] What do you think the Bone Wars were about?[2]

By the 1870s, people were very curious about dinosaurs. Charles Marsh and Edward Cope became so obsessed with fossil hunting that they started what we now call the Bone Wars.

Marsh and Cope each wanted to be the best dinosaur hunter. The men boasted about their finds. They bickered. They spied on each other, and they even stole bones from one another. For 30 years, the Bone Wars continued.

Charles Marsh

Edward Cope

What were Marsh and Cope *obsessed* about?[3] What did each man want?[4]

46

COMPREHENDING AS YOU GO

❶ **Apply:** Inferring—Topic (We will learn about the Bone Wars.)

❷ **Analyze:** Inferring (People fighting over bones—dinosaur bones . . .)

❸ **Remember:** Identifying—What; Using Vocabulary—obsessed (Marsh and Cope were obsessed with fossil hunting.)

❹ **Remember:** Identifying—Goal (They each wanted to be the best dinosaur hunter.)

Marsh and Cope were each determined to be the first to discover new kinds of dinosaurs. The two men discovered 142 new kinds of dinosaurs!

Sadly, Marsh and Cope were in such a rush to find new kinds of dinosaur bones that they were not very careful. They destroyed many bones by using dynamite to blast away rock.

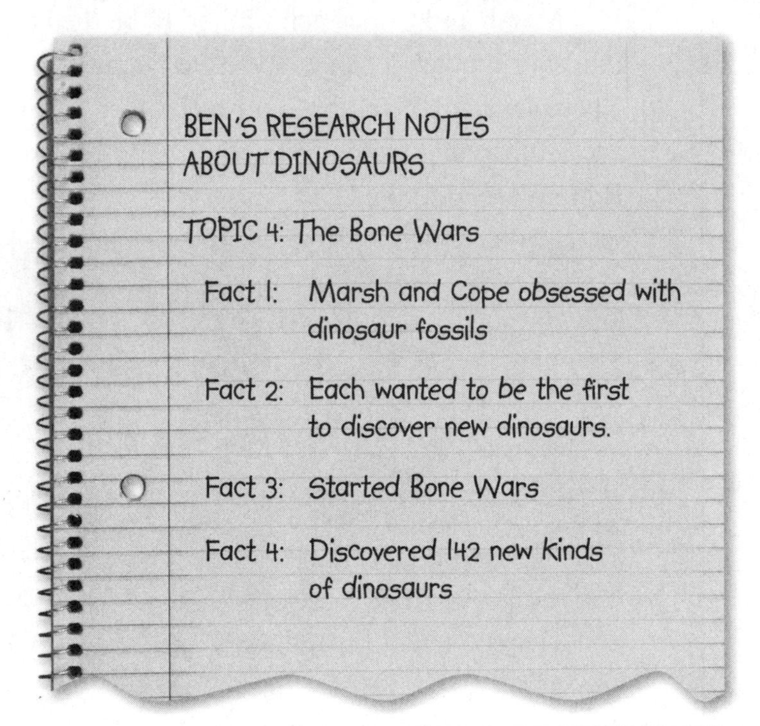

What was good about the Bone Wars? [1] What was bad about the Bone Wars? [2] Are there any facts you would add to Ben's notes to explain what the Bone Wars were? [3]

COMPREHENDING AS YOU GO

1. **Evaluate:** Making Judgments; **Understand:** Explaining (A good thing about the Bone Wars was that the two men discovered many new kinds of dinosaurs.)
2. **Evaluate:** Making Judgments; **Understand:** Explaining (A bad thing about the Bone Wars was that the two men were not careful. They destroyed a lot of bones by using dynamite . . .)
3. **Understand:** Summarizing (The men spied on each other. They stole bones from each other.)

WITH THE TEACHER

A Dinosaur Dig Today

What will we learn in this section?[1]

Now when people go on a dinosaur dig, they are very careful. They are careful not to break any of the bones. Dinosaur hunters dig out big blocks of stone, leaving the fossils untouched by shovels and picks. They put special glue on the bones and even put a coat of plaster on them. Then the fossils are carefully shipped back to a lab.

In the lab, workers carefully cut off the plaster and then use tiny picks to free the fossils from the rock. Finally, they use paintbrushes to brush off the dust.

What facts tell you that people today are very careful when they dig up dinosaur fossils?[2] Look at the picture above. What is the man in the lab doing?[3]

48

COMPREHENDING AS YOU GO

❶ **Apply:** Inferring—Topic (We will learn what happens on dinosaur digs today.)

❷ **Understand:** Identifying—Facts (Dinosaur hunters put special glue on the bones. They use tiny picks and paintbrushes to get fossils out of the rock . . .)

❸ **Apply:** Viewing, Explaining (The man is studying a dinosaur fossil . . .)

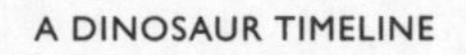

Once the bones have been carefully chipped out of the rock, scientists can study the fossils. They ask many questions. They use computers. They rebuild the dinosaur with as many real bones as possible. Using the facts they know and the facts they learn, scientists keep finding out more about these fascinating creatures.

Today, there are many places you can go to see dinosaur skeletons. People can even go on a dinosaur dig.

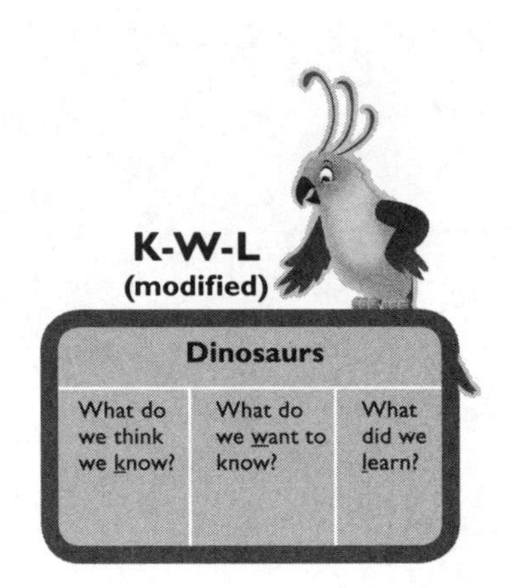

How could you find out more about dinosaurs?[1]

K-W-L CHART

Graphic Organizer; Identifying—Facts; Verifying; Asking Questions

After reading the page, have students review their K-W-L chart. While reviewing the headings and what was learned:

- put stars by facts that were verified.
- list new facts learned.
- add new questions that students may wish to research.

COMPREHENDING AS YOU GO

1 **Create:** Generating Ideas (We could go to a museum or a library. We can look them up on the Internet . . .)

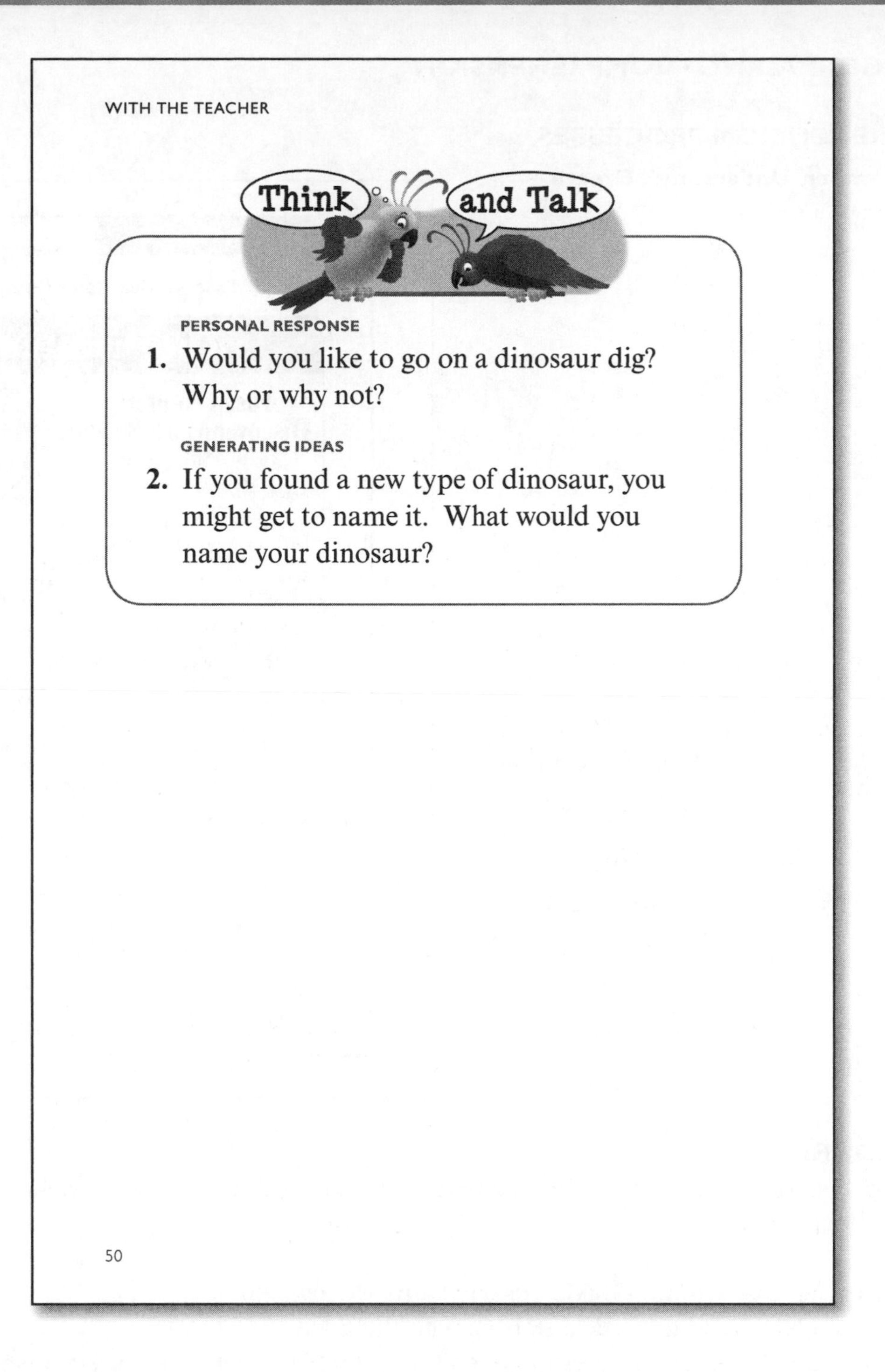

WITH THE TEACHER

Think and Talk

PERSONAL RESPONSE

1. Would you like to go on a dinosaur dig? Why or why not?

GENERATING IDEAS

2. If you found a new type of dinosaur, you might get to name it. What would you name your dinosaur?

50

❶ **Evaluate:** Responding (Yes, it would be fun because I've never seen a real dinosaur fossil. No, it would be boring because there would be a lot of digging.)

❷ **Create:** Generating Ideas (Tinasaurus, Jackosaurus, Coolosaurus . . .)

PASSAGE READING • COMPREHENSION

COMPREHENSION PROCESSES

Remember, Understand, Create

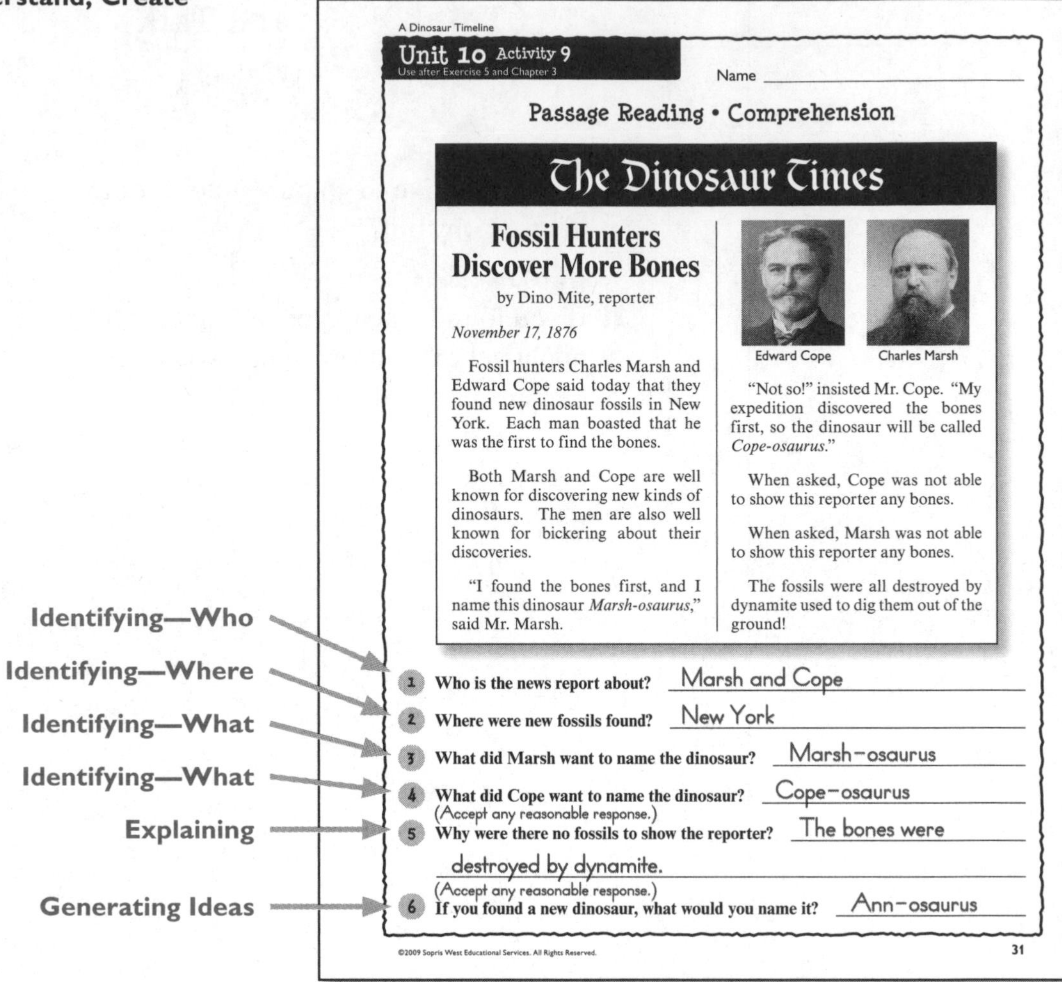

A Dinosaur Timeline

Unit 10 Activity 9
Use after Exercise 5 and Chapter 3

Name ____________________

Passage Reading • Comprehension

The Dinosaur Times

Fossil Hunters Discover More Bones

by Dino Mite, reporter

November 17, 1876

Fossil hunters Charles Marsh and Edward Cope said today that they found new dinosaur fossils in New York. Each man boasted that he was the first to find the bones.

Both Marsh and Cope are well known for discovering new kinds of dinosaurs. The men are also well known for bickering about their discoveries.

"I found the bones first, and I name this dinosaur *Marsh-osaurus*," said Mr. Marsh.

Edward Cope — Charles Marsh

"Not so!" insisted Mr. Cope. "My expedition discovered the bones first, so the dinosaur will be called *Cope-osaurus*."

When asked, Cope was not able to show this reporter any bones.

When asked, Marsh was not able to show this reporter any bones.

The fossils were all destroyed by dynamite used to dig them out of the ground!

1. Who is the news report about? Marsh and Cope
2. Where were new fossils found? New York
3. What did Marsh want to name the dinosaur? Marsh-osaurus
4. What did Cope want to name the dinosaur? Cope-osaurus
5. (Accept any reasonable response.) Why were there no fossils to show the reporter? The bones were destroyed by dynamite.
6. (Accept any reasonable response.) If you found a new dinosaur, what would you name it? Ann-osaurus

31

PROCEDURES

For each step, demonstrate and guide practice, as needed. Then have students complete the page independently.

Answering Questions—Basic Instructions (Items 1–6)

- Have students read the article starting with the title.
- Have students read each question, then fill in the blank with the correct answer.
- Think aloud with students and discuss possible answers, as needed.

Self-monitoring

Have students check and correct their work.

PERSONAL NARRATIVE • MY STORY

COMPREHENSION PROCESSES

Understand, Create

WRITING TRAITS

Ideas and Content
Word Choice
Organization—Sequencing
Conventions—Complete Sentence, Capital, Periods
Presentation

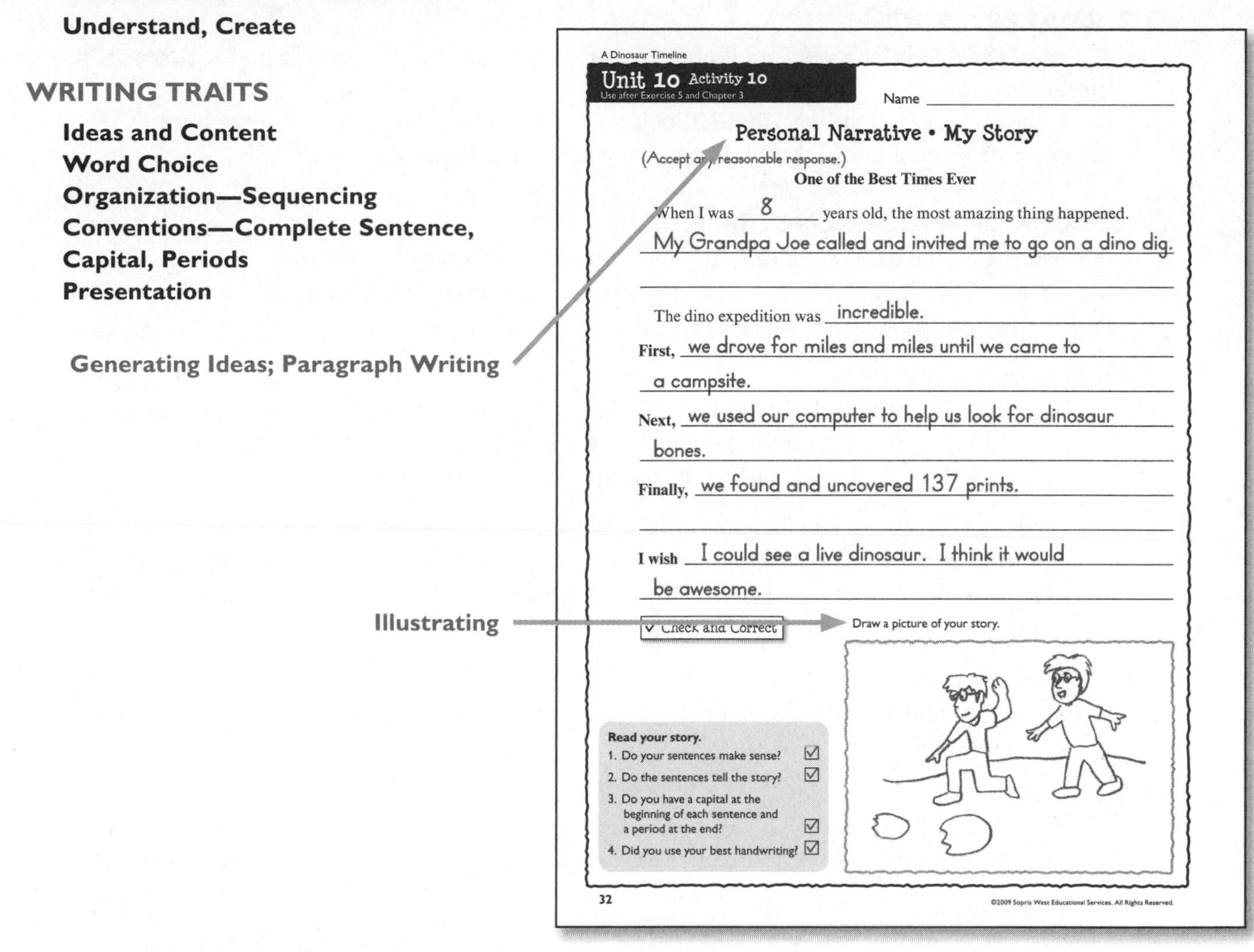

A Dinosaur Timeline

Unit 10 Activity 10
Use after Exercise 5 and Chapter 3

Name ____________________

Personal Narrative • My Story

(Accept any reasonable response.)

One of the Best Times Ever

When I was 8 years old, the most amazing thing happened.
My Grandpa Joe called and invited me to go on a dino dig.

The dino expedition was incredible.

First, we drove for miles and miles until we came to a campsite.

Next, we used our computer to help us look for dinosaur bones.

Finally, we found and uncovered 137 prints.

I wish I could see a live dinosaur. I think it would be awesome.

✓ Check and Correct

Draw a picture of your story.

Read your story.
1. Do your sentences make sense? ☑
2. Do the sentences tell the story? ☑
3. Do you have a capital at the beginning of each sentence and a period at the end? ☑
4. Did you use your best handwriting? ☑

32

©2009 Sopris West Educational Services. All Rights Reserved.

PROCEDURES

For each step, demonstrate and guide practice, as needed. Then have students complete the page independently.

1. Creative Writing: Paragraph Writing—Introductory Instructions

- Tell students they will write a fictional narrative like the one they did in the Focus Lesson. (See Exercise 5b.)
- Guide students through the activity, only as needed.
- Remind students to check and correct their work.

2. Illustrating—Basic Instructions

Have students draw a picture of their story.

❶ SOUND REVIEW

Have students read the sounds and key word phrases. Work for accuracy, then fluency.

❷ SOUND PRACTICE

- For each task, have students spell and say the focus sound in the gray bar. For Bossy E, read the header.
- Next, have students read each underlined sound, the word, then the whole column.
- Repeat with each column, building accuracy first, then fluency.

❸ ACCURACY AND FLUENCY BUILDING

- For each task, have students say any underlined part, then read the word.
- Set a pace. Then have students read the whole words in each task and column.
- Provide repeated practice, building accuracy first, then fluency.

B1. Multisyllabic Words

- For the list of words divided by syllables, have students read and finger count each syllable, then read the whole word. Use the word in a sentence, as appropriate.
- For the list of whole words, build accuracy and then fluency.

butter 2 syllables Francine likes toast with jam and . . . *butter.*
sandwich 2 syllables For lunch, Ally had a peanut butter and jelly . . . *sandwich.*
rather 2 syllables Nick didn't want to go. He said he'd . . . *rather* . . . not.
peanut 2 syllables The elephant ate a . . . *peanut.*

D1. Contractions

★Have students read each contraction and identify the words that make up the contraction.

E1. Tricky Words

- For each Tricky Word, have students use the sounds and word parts they know to silently sound out the word. Use the word in a sentence to help with pronunciation.

museum
Look at the first word. The first part is tricky. Say the word parts with me. mu-se-um
We saw lots of famous paintings at the . . . *museum.*
Read the word three times. (museum, museum, museum)

laugh The funny show made everyone . . . *laugh.*
half Please cut the sandwich in . . . *half.*
only No one else saw the shooting star. I was the . . . *only* . . . one.

- Have students read the words, building accuracy, then fluency.

E2. Story Words

Tell students the underlined sound, then have them read the word.

❹ WORDS IN CONTEXT

- Tell students to use the sounds they know and the sentence to figure out how to say each word. Assist, as needed.
- Have students read each word part, the whole word, then the sentence.

★= New in this unit

5 MORPHOGRAPHS AND AFFIXES

Have students read the underlined part, then the word.

Fluency

Unit 10 Exercise 6

Use before There's a Dinosaur in My Bed

1. SOUND REVIEW Have students review sounds for accuracy, then for fluency.

A	ow as in cow	ew as in crew	ge as in page	kn as in knee	oa as in boat
B	ci	ai	o_e	i_e	ay

2. SOUND PRACTICE In each column, have students spell and say the sound, then say any underlined sound and the word. Next, have students read the whole column.

oa	ue, ew	aw	o as in open	Bossy E
road coat roamed	Sue knew clue	lawn crawl yawned	opened cozy locate	woke games besides

3. ACCURACY AND FLUENCY BUILDING For each column, have students say any underlined part, then read each word. Next, have students read the whole column.

A1 Mixed Review	B1 Multisyllabic Words	C1 Word Endings	D1 Contractions	E1 Tricky Words
stay why soft strange towns	but•ter sand•wich rath•er pea•nut butter sandwich rather peanut	explore exploring bore boring city cities twinkle twinkled	I'd we're there's **D2** Rhyming Words picture adventure creature	museum laugh half only **E2** Story Words quiet tidy disappoint enormous

4. WORDS IN CONTEXT For each word, have students use the sounds and word parts they know to figure out the word. Then have them read the sentence.

A	moun•tains	We hiked high up into the mountains.
B	or•di•nar•y	Elizabeth wanted a fancy coat, not the same old ordinary one.
C	neigh•bor•hood	I like to go to the park in my neighborhood.
D	blan•ket	I love to wrap myself in a nice warm blanket at night.

5. MORPHOGRAPHS AND AFFIXES Have students read the underlined word part, then the word.

exclaimed	delight	unlike	biweekly	remade

24

ENTHUSIASM

Make a special effort to acknowledge what students can do.

Say things like:

You can read multisyllabic words without help from adults.

You can figure out words you've never seen before.

You can read and use snazzy words like: *museum, enormous,* and *Hadrosaurus.* That is very impressive.

FLUENCY PASSAGE INSTRUCTIONS

This Story Reading targets fluency as the primary goal of instruction and practice. Students do repeated readings of this short passage to improve accuracy, expression, and rate.

COMPREHENSION PROCESSES

Understand, Apply, Analyze

PROCEDURES

1. Warm-Up: Partner or Whisper Reading

Before beginning group Story Reading, have students finger track and partner or whisper read the selection.

2. First Reading

- Ask questions as indicated by the gray text.
- Mix group and individual turns, independent of your voice. Have students work toward a group accuracy goal of 0–4 errors. Quietly keep track of errors made by all students in the group.
- After reading the story, practice any difficult words. Reread the story if students have not reached the accuracy goal.

3. Second Reading, Short Passage Practice: Developing Prosody

- Demonstrate reading the first paragraph with expression and fluency. Have students finger track as you read.
- Have students choral read the first paragraph. Encourage reading with expression and fluency.
- Repeat with the second paragraph.

4. Third Reading, Group Timed Readings: Repeated Reading

- Select a page. Encourage each child to work for a personal best. Have students whisper read for a one-minute Timed Reading. Tell students to go back to the top of the page and keep reading until the minute is up.
- Have students put their finger on the last word they read and count the number of words read correctly in one minute.
- Have students do a second Timed Reading of the same page.
- Have students try to beat their last score.
- Celebrate improvements.

5. Written Assessment (Comprehension and Skill)

Tell students they will do a Written Assessment after they read "There's a Dinosaur in My Bed" (For teacher directions, see pages 102 and 103.)

6. Homework 6: Repeated Reading

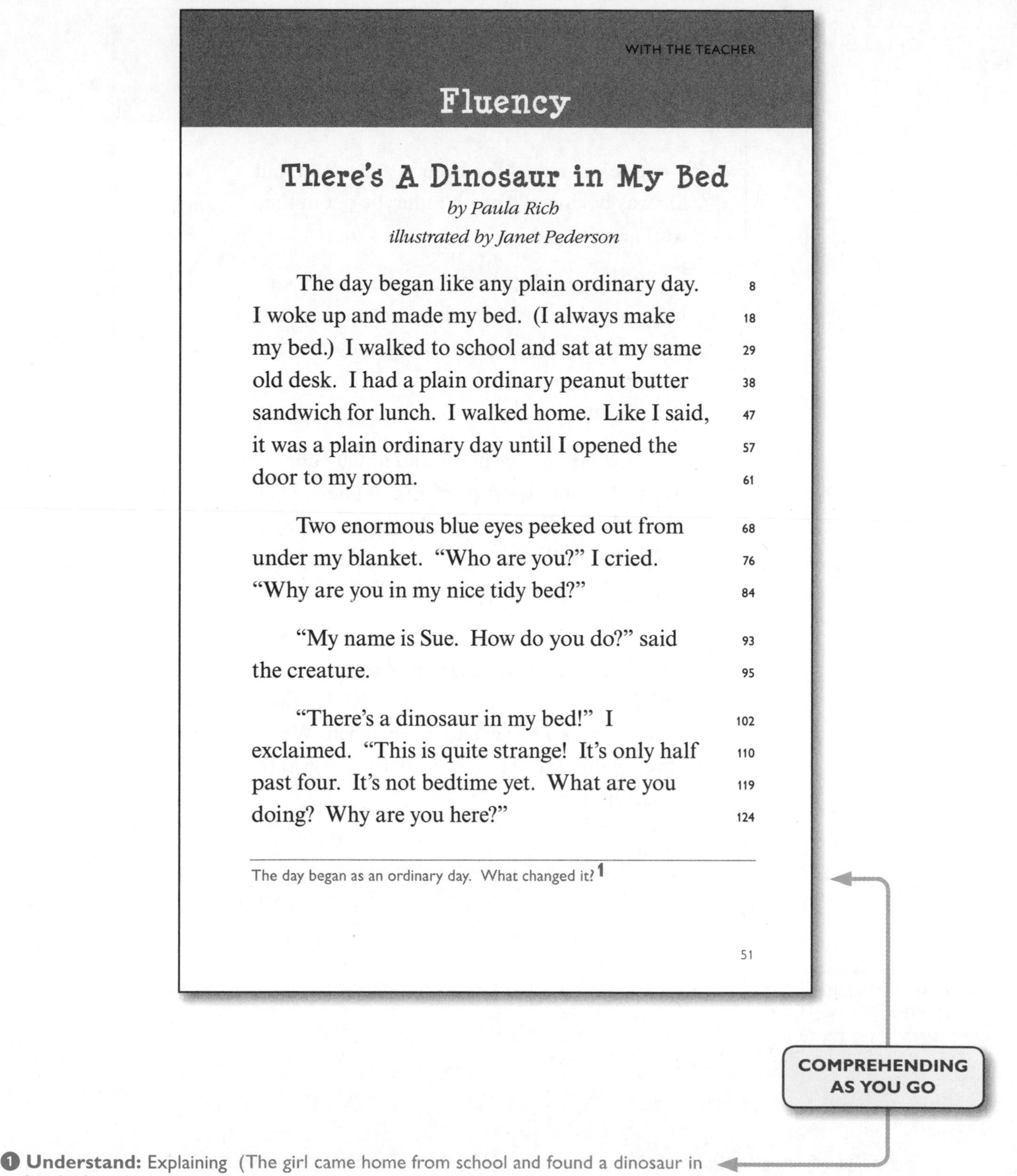

WITH THE TEACHER

Fluency

There's A Dinosaur in My Bed

by Paula Rich

illustrated by Janet Pederson

The day began like any plain ordinary day. I woke up and made my bed. (I always make my bed.) I walked to school and sat at my same old desk. I had a plain ordinary peanut butter sandwich for lunch. I walked home. Like I said, it was a plain ordinary day until I opened the door to my room. 8 18 29 38 47 57 61

Two enormous blue eyes peeked out from under my blanket. "Who are you?" I cried. "Why are you in my nice tidy bed?" 68 76 84

"My name is Sue. How do you do?" said the creature. 93 95

"There's a dinosaur in my bed!" I exclaimed. "This is quite strange! It's only half past four. It's not bedtime yet. What are you doing? Why are you here?" 102 110 119 124

The day began as an ordinary day. What changed it? [1]

51

COMPREHENDING AS YOU GO

1 **Understand:** Explaining (The girl came home from school and found a dinosaur in her bed . . .)

WITH THE TEACHER

Fluency

Sue yawned. "I've been in a museum, but life was boring. I'd much rather be out in the world exploring! 8 18 20

"So one night I just walked out the door. No more plain ordinary days for this dinosaur. I roamed through forests and mountains, cities and towns. What fun! But finally I began to slow down. 29 37 44 53 55

"I came to your house and found your cozy soft bed. A nice quiet place to call home, I said! So that's why I'm here, and I hope I can stay. I'm clean and I'm neat—please don't send me away!" Sue's big blue eyes twinkled. 64 75 86 95 101

How can you disappoint a dinosaur? Sue stayed. I'm the only kid in the neighborhood with a dinosaur for a best friend. We laugh, play games, and go exploring together. We're never plain. We're never ordinary. Every day is an adventure! 108 116 125 132 140 142

Why did the girl let Sue stay?[1] Why is every day an *adventure?*[2]

52

COMPREHENDING AS YOU GO

1. **Apply:** Inferring; Using Vocabulary—**disappoint** (The girl let Sue stay because she couldn't disappoint a dinosaur. She felt sorry for Sue. Sue asked very nicely if she could stay.)
2. **Analyze:** Inferring; **Apply:** Using Vocabulary—**adventure, ordinary** (Every day is an adventure because doing things with a dinosaur is never ordinary . . .)

THERE'S A DINOSAUR IN MY BED
53

WRITTEN ASSESSMENT

COMPREHENSION PROCESSES

Remember, Understand, Apply

WRITING TRAITS

Ideas and Content
Word Choice
Conventions—Complete Sentence, Capital, Period
Presentation

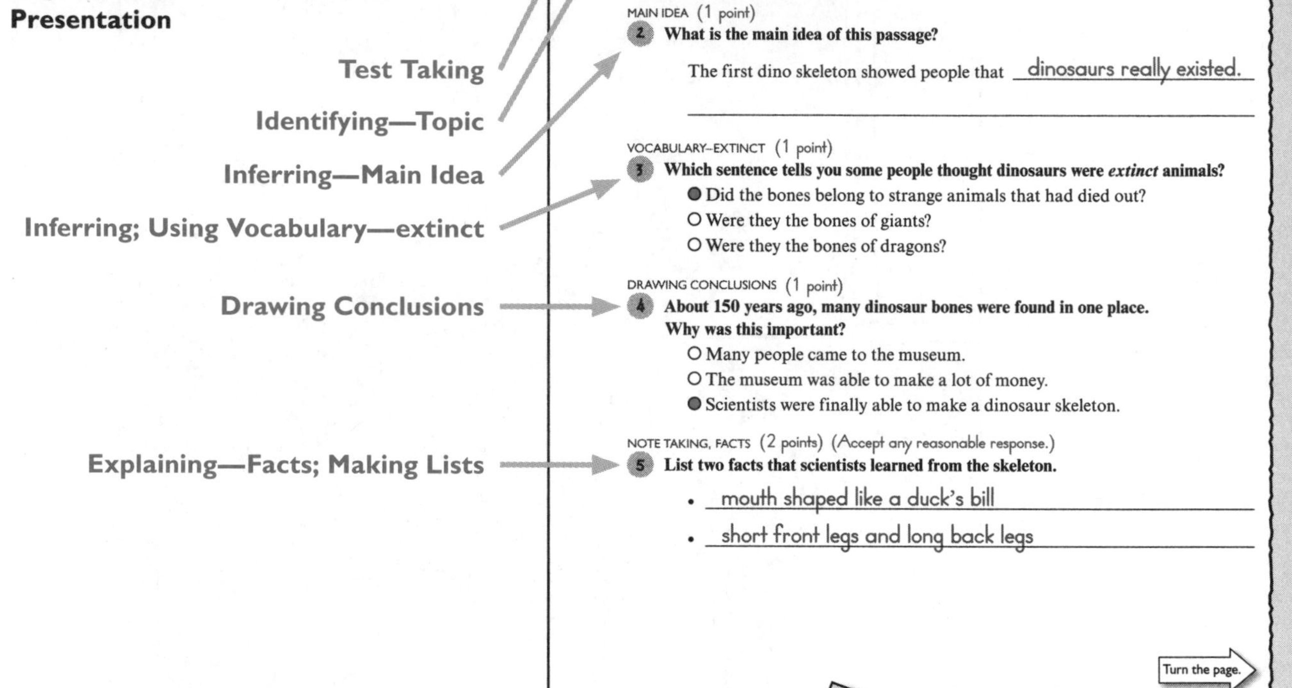

Unit 10 Written Assessment (continued)

TOPIC (1 point)

1. **What is the passage about?**
   - O New Jersey
   - O the Bone Wars
   - ● the first dinosaur skeleton

MAIN IDEA (1 point)

2. **What is the main idea of this passage?**

   The first dino skeleton showed people that dinosaurs really existed.

VOCABULARY–EXTINCT (1 point)

3. **Which sentence tells you some people thought dinosaurs were *extinct* animals?**
   - ● Did the bones belong to strange animals that had died out?
   - O Were they the bones of giants?
   - O Were they the bones of dragons?

DRAWING CONCLUSIONS (1 point)

4. **About 150 years ago, many dinosaur bones were found in one place. Why was this important?**
   - O Many people came to the museum.
   - O The museum was able to make a lot of money.
   - ● Scientists were finally able to make a dinosaur skeleton.

NOTE TAKING, FACTS (2 points) (Accept any reasonable response.)

5. **List two facts that scientists learned from the skeleton.**
   - mouth shaped like a duck's bill
   - short front legs and long back legs

Turn the page.

©2009 Sopris West Educational Services. All Rights Reserved. 69

PROCEDURES

Do not demonstrate or guide practice.

Written Assessment—Introductory Instructions

1. Introduce the Written Assessment.
   - Remind students that their work today is an opportunity for them to show what they can do independently. Clarify your expectations, as needed.
   - Tell students they will whisper read the passage and then answer the questions without help.

Unit 10 Written Assessment

WARM-UP

beast New Jersey skeleton

The First Dinosaur Skeleton

For hundreds of years, people found huge bones. These bones were found one at a time. No one knew what they were. Were they the bones of giants? Were they the bones of dragons? Did the bones belong to strange animals that had died out?

About 150 years ago, many bones were found in one place. They were found in New Jersey. People were excited. For the first time, scientists were able to put together the body of a dinosaur. They were able to build a dino skeleton.

When the skeleton was finished, they put it in a museum. Thousands of people came to see it. They were amazed. The dino was 23 feet long and 10 feet tall. It had short front legs, and it walked on its long back legs. Its mouth was shaped like a duck's bill. For the first time, people knew that dinosaurs were real. Huge extinct beasts had once roamed the world.

68

continued

WRITTEN ASSESSMENT (*continued*)

Responding, Generating Ideas, Sentence Completion, Sentence Writing

Unit 10 Written Assessment
(continued)

PERSONAL RESPONSE (2 points) (Accept any reasonable response.)

6 What would you do if you found a dinosaur bone? Write at least two sentences.

If I found a dinosaur bone, first I would wrap it up carefully and take it to a museum.

Then I would have the bone looked at by a scientist so that I could find out what type of dinosaur it was.

✓ Check and Correct

Reread your answers.
Do your answers make sense? ☑
Do you have a capital at the beginning of each sentence and a period at the end? ☑
Did you use your best handwriting? ☑

SCORING Date ____________

Topic 1 /1 Main Idea 1 /1 Vocabulary 1 /1
Drawing Conclusions 1 /1 Facts 2 /2 Personal Response 2 /2 Total 8 /8

Teachers: If you wish to keep a cumulative record of student assessment scores, see the *Assessment Manual.*

70

2. Check for student understanding.
   Say something like:
   Look at your assessment. What are you going to do first? (write my name)

   What are going to do next? (whisper read the passage)
   What will you do after you read the passage? (answer the questions)

   That's great. Now what will you do if you get to a hard question?
   (reread the question and try again)
   That's right. What should you do if it's still hard? (reread the passage and try again)
   Very good. And if you still aren't sure, what will you do? (do my best and keep going)

3. Remind students to check and correct.
   When you finish your assessment, what should you do? (check and correct)
   That's right. Go to the top of the page. Reread the questions and make sure your answers make sense. Fix anything that doesn't sound right. Make sure you have an answer for every question.

4. Remind students what to do when they finish their work.

End of the Unit

In this section, you will find:

Making Decisions

As you near the end of the unit, plan to give the Written Assessment and the Oral Reading Fluency Assessment to each child in your group. Use this section as a general guide for making instructional decisions and doing diagnostic planning.

Written Assessment

The Unit 10 Written Assessment is located on page 67 of the Activity Book and on the CD.

Oral Reading Fluency Assessment

The Unit 10 Oral Reading Fluency Assessment is located on page 108 of this teacher's guide and in the *Assessment Manual.*

Certificate of Achievement

Celebrate your children's accomplishments. When your students master the unit skills, send home the Certificate of Achievement. Have students set goals for the next unit.

Extra Practice Lessons

Use the Extra Practice lessons for students who need additional decoding and fluency work. Student materials can be copied from the Extra Practice blackline masters.

Making Decisions

GENERAL ASSESSMENT GUIDELINES

1. After students read Story Reading 6, "There's a Dinosaur in My Bed," give the group the Unit 10 Written Assessment in place of Comprehension and Skill Work. Follow the instructions on pages 102 and 103 of this guide.

2. While the group is completing the Written Assessment or any time during the day, administer the Oral Reading Fluency Assessment. Assess each student individually.

   Optional: Graph the results of the assessment. (See Unit 7 Teacher's Guide, pages 92 and 95.)
   - If the student's words correct per minute go up, congratulate the student.
   - If the student's words correct per minute go down, discuss the student's overall improvement and help him or her identify ways to improve for the next assessment.

3. Score oral fluency responses on the Student Assessment Record. Adhere to the scoring criteria in the *Assessment Manual.* Use a stopwatch to time how long it takes each student to read the Oral Reading Fluency Passage, and record errors.

USING THE WRITTEN ASSESSMENT RESULTS

Results of the Written Assessment *should not* be used to determine whether a student or group of students continues forward in the program. As long as students pass the Oral Reading Fluency Assessment, they should continue forward with the next unit.

The Written Assessment should be used to informally monitor how well students read independently and answer questions in writing. If any student has difficulty with the Written Assessment, re-administer the assessment orally.

If the student has difficulty answering the questions orally:
- Record the types of errors (e.g., main idea, sequencing, open-ended response).
- Provide explicit instruction for these types of questions during reading group, before independent work, and in tutorials, as needed.
  1) Demonstrate (or model) appropriate responses, guide practice, and provide opportunities for independent practice.
  2) For inferential questions, think aloud with students—explain how you arrive at an answer.
  3) For literal questions, teach students to reread a passage, locate information, reread the question, and respond.

At this level, if the student is able to answer the questions orally but not on paper, it may not be due to comprehension problems. The student's difficulties may be related to a lack of motivation, an inability to work independently, or a struggle with handwriting, spelling, language, or vocabulary.

USING THE ORAL READING FLUENCY RESULTS

At the end of each unit, you will need to make decisions regarding student progress. Should students go forward in the program? Does the group need Extra Practice before proceeding?

Do individuals require more assistance and practice to continue working in their group? These decisions all require use of the oral reading fluency data and professional judgment. As you analyze assessment results, watch for trends and anomalies.

See the *Assessment Manual* for detailed information and instructional recommendations. General guidelines and recommendations follow:

Score	Recommendations
Strong Pass ≥ 110 WCPM 0–2 errors	• Continue with the current pace of instruction. • Have students set goals. (Until students are reading approximately 180 words correct per minute, oral reading fluency continues to be an instructional goal.)
Pass 88–109 WCPM 0–2 errors	• Continue with the current pace of instruction. Consider increasing fluency practice.
No Pass ≤ 87 WCPM	• If a child scores a No Pass but has previously passed all assessments, you may wish to advance the student to the next unit, then carefully monitor the student. • If a child scores a No Pass but has previously passed all assessments, you may wish to advance the student to the next unit and also provide additional practice opportunities. (See below.) • If a child scores two consecutive No Passes or periodic No Passes, additional practice must be provided. (See below.) • If a child scores three consecutive No Passes, the student should be placed in a lower-performing group.

RED FLAG

A No Pass is a red flag. A mild early intervention can prevent an intense and time-consuming intervention in the future.

Added Practice Options for Groups

Warm-Ups:

- Begin each lesson with Partner Reading of the previous day's homework.
- Begin each day with Partner Reading of a Word Fluency from Extra Practice.
- Begin each lesson with a five-minute Fluency Booster. Place copies of the Unit 1–9 *Read Well* Homework in three-ring notebooks. Each day, have students begin Finger Tracking and Whisper Reading at Unit 1, Homework 1. At the end of five minutes, have students mark where they are in their notebooks. The next day, the goal is to read farther.
- Begin each Story Reading with a review of the previous day's story.
- After reading the story, include Short Passage Practice on a daily basis.

Extended Units: If several children begin to score No Passes or barely pass, extend the unit by adding Extra Practices 1, 2, and/or 3. Extra Practice lessons include Decoding Practice, Fluency Passage, Word Fluency, and a Comprehension and Skill Activity. (See pages 110–115 in this guide.)

Jell-Well Reviews: A Jell-Well Review is the *Read Well* term for a review of earlier units. A Jell-Well Review is a period of time taken to celebrate what children have learned and an opportunity to firm up their foundation of learning. To complete a Jell-Well Review, take the group back to the last unit for which all students scored Strong Passes. Then quickly cycle back up. See the *Assessment Manual* for how to build a Jell-Well Review.

Added Practice Options for Individual Students

Tutorials: Set up five-minute tutorials on a daily basis with an assistant, trained volunteer, or cross-age tutor. Have the tutor provide Short Passage Practice and Timed Readings or Extra Practice lessons.

Double Dose: Find ways to provide a double dose of *Read Well* instruction.

- Have the student work in his or her group *and* a lower-performing group.
- Have an instructional assistant, older student, or parent volunteer preview or review lessons.
- Have an instructional assistant provide instruction with Extra Practice lessons.
- Preview new lessons or review previous lessons.

END-OF-THE-UNIT CELEBRATION

When students pass the Oral Reading Fluency Assessment, celebrate with the Certificate of Achievement on page 109.

Note: Using the Flesch-Kincaid Grade Level readability formula, the Unit 10 Assessment has a 2.5 readability level. Readability formulas provide only a rough estimate of difficulty. Just adding one or two multisyllabic words to the passage can increase the readability by one or two months.

TRICKY WORD and FOCUS SKILL WARM-UP

soap	watched	whole	read	picture	front

ORAL READING FLUENCY PASSAGE

A Dream of Dinosaurs

★Ralph was a curious little boy. He wanted to know 10
about everything. 12

"Why are there stars in the sky?" Ralph asked his mother. 23
Ralph's mother bought him a book about stars. Ralph read the 34
whole book from front to back. 40

Ralph asked his father, "How does a computer work?" 49
Ralph's father took him to a lab. A scientist explained how the 61
computers work. 63

"Why does soap float?" Ralph asked his sister. His sister 73
said, "Don't ask me! Go ask Grandpa." Grandpa helped Ralph 83
learn about soap on the computer. 89

Ralph wanted to know about dinosaurs too. He read 98
many books about them. He watched some shows on TV about 109
dinosaurs. Then Ralph decided to write his own book. He wrote 120
down all he knew about dinosaurs. He drew pictures of them. He 132
showed his family the book. Everyone was impressed. 140

ORAL READING FLUENCY Start timing at the ★. Mark errors. Make a single slash in the text (/) at 60 seconds. Have the student complete the passage. If the student completes the passage in less than 60 seconds, have the student go back to the ★ and continue reading. Make a double slash (//) in the text at 60 seconds.

WCPM Determine words correct per minute by subtracting errors from words read in 60 seconds.

STRONG PASS The student scores no more than 2 errors on the first pass through the passage and reads 110 or more words correct per minute. Proceed to Unit 11.

PASS The student scores no more than 2 errors on the first pass through the passage and reads 88 to 109 words correct per minute. Proceed to Unit 11.

NO PASS The student scores 3 or more errors on the first pass through the passage and/or reads 87 or fewer words correct per minute. Provide added fluency practice with RW2 Unit 10 Extra Practice. (Lessons follow the certificate at the end of the teacher's guide.) After completing the Extra Practice, retest the student.

Something to ROAR About!

____

has successfully completed

Read Well* 2 Unit 10 • *Dino Discoveries

with ______ words correct per minute.

Teacher Signature ____________________________

Date ___________________________________

Something to ROAR About!

____

has successfully completed

Read Well* 2 Unit 10 • *Dino Discoveries

with ______ words correct per minute.

Teacher Signature ____________________________

Date ___________________________________

PROCEDURES

1. Sound Review
Use selected Sound Cards from Units 1–10.

2. Sounding Out Smoothly
- For each word, have students say the underlined part, sound out the word smoothly, then read the whole word. Use the words in sentences, as needed.
- Repeat practice. Mix group and individual turns, independent of your voice.

3. Accuracy and Fluency Building
- For each task, have students say any underlined part, then read each word.
- Set a pace. Then have students read the whole words in each task and column.
- Repeat practice, building accuracy first, then fluency.

4. Tricky Words
Have students read each row for accuracy, then fluency.

EXTRA PRACTICE 1

Unit 10 Decoding Practice

Name ____________________

1. SOUND REVIEW Use selected Sound Cards from Units 1–10.

2. SOUNDING OUT SMOOTHLY Have students say the underlined part, sound out and read each word, then read the row.

tracks	row	Dave	Rich

3. ACCURACY/FLUENCY BUILDING Have students say any underlined part, then read each word. Next, have students read the column.

A1 Sound Practice	B1 Word Endings	C1 Rhyming Words	D1 Contractions
boat soap float roam	excite exciting grab grabbed	more shore before	let's don't wasn't
A2 Compound Words		**C2** Bossy E	**D2** Sound Practice
footprints riverbank rowboat	quickly jumped noticed watched walked wanted	life line holes bones	ago about along again around

4. TRICKY WORDS Have students read each row for accuracy, then fluency.

A	boys	spread	dinosaur	friend	millions	5
B	lived	front	school	word	area	10

5. MULTISYLLABIC WORDS Have students read the word by parts, tell how many syllables are in the word, then read the whole word.

A	Jus•tin	Justin	jack•ets	jackets
B	Ne•bras•ka	Nebraska	sci•en•tist	scientist
C	shal•low	shallow	def•i•nite•ly	definitely

6. DICTATION Say the word. Have students say the word, then finger count and say the sounds. Have students say each sound as they touch or write it.

A1 Shifty Words	B1 Rhyming Words
kn ow kn ew d r ew	l oo k b oo k t oo k

 64

CAUTION
Your children may not need Extra Practice. Use assessment results to determine if Extra Practice is needed.

5. Multisyllabic Words
For each word, have students read each syllable out loud, finger count the syllables, then tell how many syllables are in the word. If needed, use the word in a sentence. Have students read the whole word.

6. Dictation

know, knew, drew, look, book, took
- Say "know." Have students say the word. Guide students as they finger count and say the sounds. Have students touch or write the sounds, then read the word. Say something like:

  The first word is ***know.*** Say the word. (know) Say and count the sounds in ***know*** with me. **Hold up one finger for each sound.** /nnn/•/ōōō/ How many sounds? (two)
  What's the first sound? (/nnn/) Touch under /nnn/.
  What's the next sound? (/ōōō/) Write /ōōō/ with the o-w pattern.
  Read the word. (know)
- Repeat with "knew" and "drew."
- Continue with the rhyming words: look, book, took.

PROCEDURES

1. **First Reading**
   Have students work toward an accuracy goal of 0–2 errors and practice any difficult words.

2. **Second Reading, Short Passage Practice: Developing Prosody**
   - Demonstrate how to read a line or two.
   - Guide practice with your voice.
   - Provide individual turns while others track with their fingers and whisper read.

3. **Partner Reading: Repeated Reading (Checkout Opportunity)**

   While students do Partner Reading, listen to individuals read the passage. Work on accuracy and fluency, as needed.

4. **Homework: Repeated Reading**

EXTRA PRACTICE 1

Unit 10 Fluency Passage

Name ____________

Fluency Passage

My goal is to read with 0–2 errors and ___ words correct per minute.

I read with ___ errors and ___ words correct per minute.

Justin's Discovery

"Let's go floating down the river again," said Justin to his friend Dave. The boys lived in a small town in Nebraska. Floating down the river in a rowboat was fun! (12, 25, 31)

The boys grabbed their life jackets and jumped in the boat. They floated for a long time, then rowed to shore. As they walked along the riverbank, they noticed a line of shallow holes in the ground. (43, 57, 68)

"Dinosaur footprints!" said Justin. (72)

Word about the footprints spread. All their friends from school wanted to see them. (82, 86)

"Definitely dinosaur footprints," their friend Rich said. He looked around the area and found a bone too. "Let's show my dad what we found. He knows a scientist." It wasn't long before the kids found more tracks and more bones. It was exciting to think that dinosaurs roamed this area millions of years ago. (95, 109, 122, 134, 140)

Homework

I've listened to my child read this p... Signed ____________

65

Unit 10 Activity

Passage Comprehension

Justin's Discovery

1. What made the boys think they had found dinosaur footprints?
   - ○ They noticed footprints in their boat as they were floating down the creek.
   - ● They noticed a line of shallow holes in the ground along the riverbank.
   - ○ They noticed footprints in the creek as they were floating in their boat.
2. Rich wanted to show his dad what they had found. Why?
   He wanted to show his dad because his dad knows a scientist.
3. How did the kids feel about finding more tracks and more bones?
   The kids were excited.

Paragraph Comprehension

Long ago, four scientists floated down ... hunted for dinosaur fossils along the riverb... dinosaurs. Most of the dinosaurs were new...

1. Where did the scientists hunt for dinosaur...
   Scientists hunted for dinosaur...
2. Most of the dinosaur fossils that scientists fo...
   - ○ not new to scientists
   - ● new to scientists
   - ○ floating down the river

Unit 10 Word Fluency A

Rhyming Words

roast	toast	coast	boast	seacoast
think	stink	blink	drink	rethink
tab	grab	stab	crab	taxicab
ice	nice	twice	slice	advice
braid	paid	maid	laid	afraid

Related Words

locate	located	relocate	dislocate	location
determine	determined	determining	undetermined	determination
miss	missed	missing	dismiss	dismissed
define	defined	defines	definition	definitely
imagine	imagined	imagining	imagination	imaginative

High-Frequency Tricky Words

something	example	begin	those
begin	those	something	both
those	begin	both	example
both	something	example	begin
example	both	those	something

PROCEDURES • ACTIVITY AND WORD FLUENCY A

Demonstrate and guide practice, as needed.

1. **Activity**
   Passage Comprehension
   - Have students read each sentence or question, then fill in the bubble and/or blank with the correct answer.
   - Think aloud with students and discuss the multiple-choice options, as needed.

   Paragraph Comprehension
   - Have students read the paragraph.
   - Have students read each numbered sentence, then fill in the bubble and/or blank.
   - Have students read the completed sentences.

2. **Word Fluency (BLMs are located on the CD.)**
   - To build fluency, have students read each section three times in a row.
   - To build accuracy, have students read all sets with partners.

PROCEDURES

1. Sound Review

Use selected Sound Cards from Units 1–10.

2. Sounding Out Smoothly

- For each word, have students say the underlined part, sound out the word smoothly, then read the whole word. Use the words in sentences, as needed.
- Repeat practice. Mix group and individual turns.

3. Accuracy and Fluency Building

- For each task, have students say any underlined part, then read each word.
- Set a pace. Then have students read the whole words in each task and column.
- Provide repeated practice, building accuracy first, then fluency.

4. Tricky Words

Have students read each row for accuracy, then fluency.

EXTRA PRACTICE 2

Unit 10 Decoding Practice

Name ____________________

1. SOUND REVIEW Use selected Sound Cards from Units 1–10.

2. SOUNDING OUT SMOOTHLY Have students say the underlined part, sound out and read each word, then read the row.

soap	show	dream	now

3. ACCURACY/FLUENCY BUILDING Have students say any underlined part, then read each word. Next, have students read the column.

A1 Mixed Practice	B1 Buildups	C1 Related Words	D1 Rhyming Words
today over leader summer explained excited decided showed turned impressed	cover discover discovered **B2 Compound Words** footprints sometimes everyone everything faraway someday	know knew write wrote become became **C2 Bossy E** takes places hikes	kind find mind **D2 Tricky Words** spread read head full work word

4. TRICKY WORDS Have students read each row for accuracy, then fluency.

A	goes	bought	people	father	does	5
B	eight	ones	because	learn	curious	10

5. MULTISYLLABIC WORDS Have students read the word by parts, tell how many syllables are in the word, then read the whole word.

A	fos•sils	fossils	mu•se•um	museum
B	com•put•ers	computers	ex•pe•di•tion	expedition

6. DICTATION Say the word. Have students say the word, then finger count and say the sounds. Have students say each sound as they touch or write it.

A1 Shifty Words	B1 Rhyming Words
h o p e	f l oa t
h o m e	b oa t
h i m	c oa t

 67

CAUTION

Your children may not need Extra Practice. Use assessment results to determine if Extra Practice is needed.

5. Multisyllabic Words

For each word, have students read each syllable out loud, finger count the syllables, then tell how many syllables are in the word. If needed, use the word in a sentence. Have students read the whole word.

6. Dictation

hope, home, him, float, boat, coat

- Say "light." Have students say the word. Guide students as they finger count and say the sounds. Have students touch or write the sounds, then read the word.

  The first word is ***hope.*** Say the word. (hope)

  Say and count the sounds in ***hope*** with me.

  Hold up one finger for each sound. /h/•/ōōō/•/p/ How many sounds? (three)

  What's the first sound? (/h/) Touch under /h/.

  What's the next sound? (/ōōō/) Write (ōōō).

  What's the last sound? (/p/) Touch under /p/.

  The Bossy E at the end makes o say its name. Read the word. (hope)

- Repeat with "home" and "him."
- Continue with the rhyming words: float, boat, coat.

PROCEDURES

1. **First Reading**
   Have students work toward an accuracy goal of 0–2 errors and practice any difficult words.

2. **Second Reading, Timed Reading: Repeated Reading**
   - Once the group accuracy goal has been achieved, time individual students for 30 or 60 seconds while the other children track with their fingers and whisper read.
   - Determine WCPM. Celebrate when students reach their goals!

3. **Partner Reading: Repeated Reading (Checkout Opportunity)**
   While students do Partner Reading, listen to individuals read the passage. Work on accuracy and fluency, as needed.

4. **Homework: Repeated Reading**

PROCEDURES • ACTIVITY AND WORD FLUENCY B

Demonstrate and guide practice, as needed.

1. **Activity**
   Passage Comprehension
   - Have students read each question, then fill in the bubble or blank with the correct answer.
   - Think aloud with students and discuss the multiple-choice options, as needed.

   Paragraph Comprehension
   - Have students read the paragraph.
   - Have students read each numbered sentence, then fill in the bubble and/or blank.
   - Have students read the completed sentences.

   Self-monitoring
   Have students read and check their work.

2. **Word Fluency (BLMs are located on the CD.)**
   - To build fluency, have students read each section three times in a row.
   - To build accuracy, have students read all sets with partners.

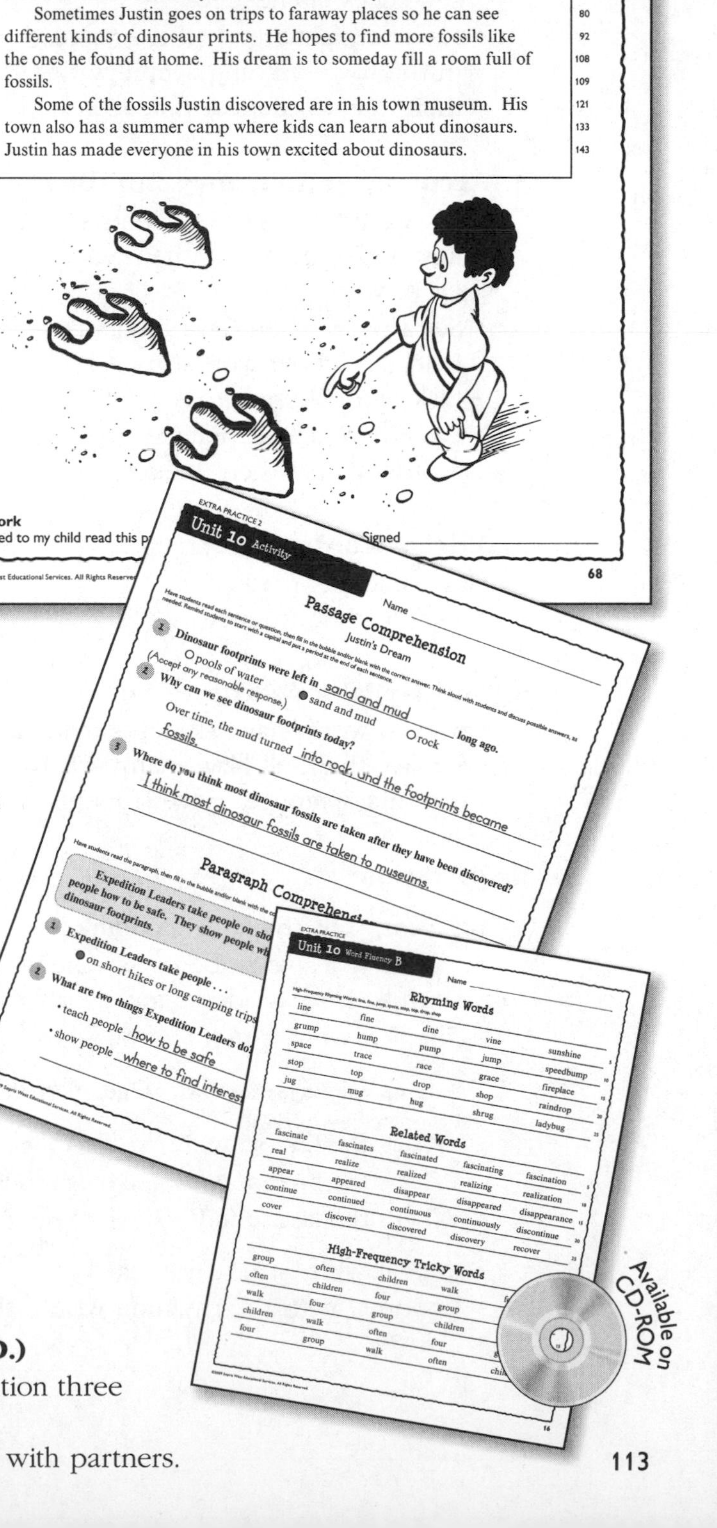

EXTRA PRACTICE 2

Unit 10 Fluency Passage

Name ____________

Fluency Passage

My goal is to read with 0–2 errors and ___ words correct per minute.

I read with ___ errors and ___ words correct per minute.

Justin's Dream

Justin was eight years old when he and his friend Dave found	12
dinosaur footprints. Now Justin works at the museum and is an	23
Expedition Leader. He takes people on hikes to see the footprints.	34
The dinosaur footprints that Justin found were left in sand and	45
mud long ago. Over time, the mud turned into rock, and the footprints	58
became fossils. This is why we can see them today.	68
Sometimes Justin goes on trips to faraway places so he can see	80
different kinds of dinosaur prints. He hopes to find more fossils like	92
the ones he found at home. His dream is to someday fill a room full of	108
fossils.	109
Some of the fossils Justin discovered are in his town museum. His	121
town also has a summer camp where kids can learn about dinosaurs.	133
Justin has made everyone in his town excited about dinosaurs.	143

Homework
I've listened to my child read this p... Signed ____________

68

Unit 10 Activity

Passage Comprehension
Justin's Dream

1. Dinosaur footprints were left in sand and mud long ago.
   ○ pools of water ● sand and mud ○ rock
   (Accept any reasonable response.)
2. Why can we see dinosaur footprints today?
   Over time, the mud turned into rock, and the footprints became fossils.
3. Where do you think most dinosaur fossils are taken after they have been discovered?
   I think most dinosaur fossils are taken to museums.

Paragraph Comprehension

Expedition Leaders take people on sho... people how to be safe. They show people wh... dinosaur footprints.

1. Expedition Leaders take people . . .
   ● on short hikes or long camping trips
2. What are two things Expedition Leaders do?
   • teach people how to be safe
   • show people where to find interes...

Unit 10 Word Fluency B

Rhyming Words

line	fine	dine	vine	sunshine
grump	bump	pump	jump	speedbump
space	trace	race	grace	fireplace
stop	top	drop	shop	raindrop
jug	mug	hug	shrug	ladybug

Related Words

fascinate	fascinates	fascinated	fascinating	fascination
real	realize	realized	realizing	realization
appear	appeared	disappear	disappeared	disappearance
continue	continued	continuous	continuously	discontinue
cover	discover	discovered	discovery	recover

High-Frequency Tricky Words

group	often	children	walk
often	children	four	group
walk	four	group	children
children	walk	often	four
four	group	walk	often

PROCEDURES

1. Sound Review

Use selected Sound Cards from Units 1–10.

2. Sounding Out Smoothly

- For each word, have students say the underlined part, sound out the word smoothly, then read the whole word. Use the words in sentences, as needed.
- Have students read all the words in the row, building accuracy first, then fluency. Repeat practice.

3. Accuracy and Fluency Building

- For each task, have students say any underlined part, then read each word.
- Set a pace. Then have students read the whole words in each task and column.
- Provide repeated practice, building accuracy first, then fluency.

4. Tricky Words

Have students read each row for accuracy, then fluency.

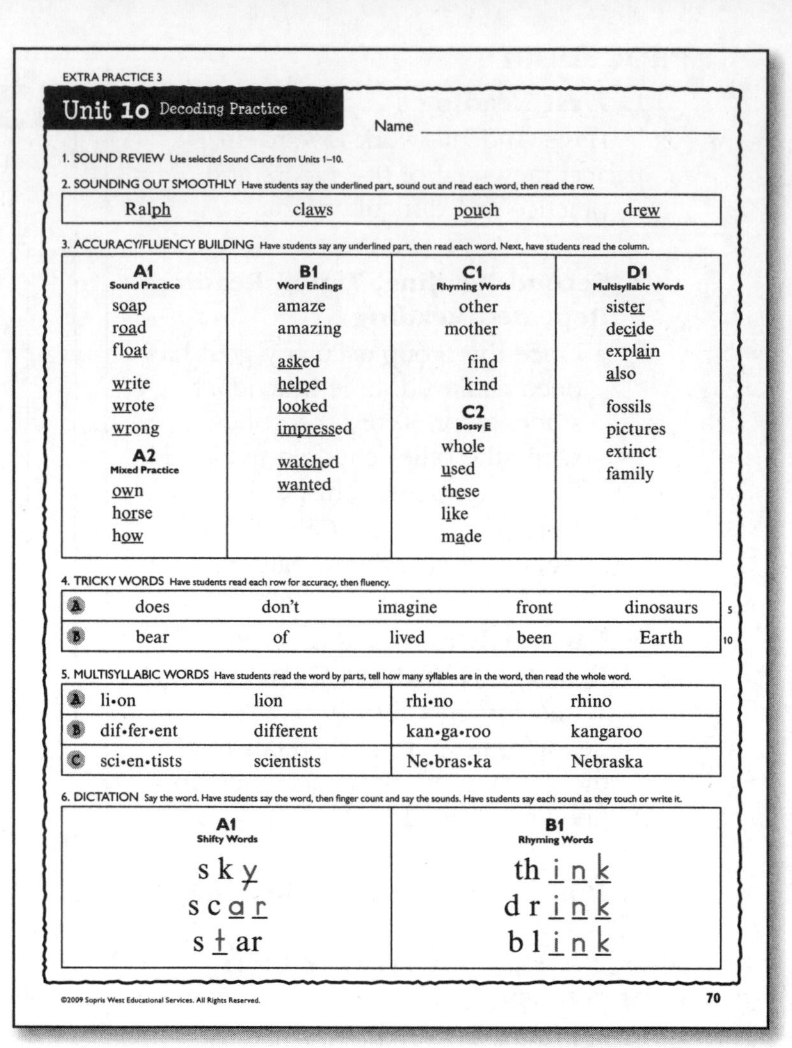

EXTRA PRACTICE 3

Unit 10 Decoding Practice

Name ____________________

1. SOUND REVIEW Use selected Sound Cards from Units 1–10.

2. SOUNDING OUT SMOOTHLY Have students say the underlined part, sound out and read each word, then read the row.

Ralph	claws	pouch	drew

3. ACCURACY/FLUENCY BUILDING Have students say any underlined part, then read each word. Next, have students read the column.

A1 Sound Practice	B1 Word Endings	C1 Rhyming Words	D1 Multisyllabic Words
soap road float write wrote wrong **A2** Mixed Practice own horse how	amaze amazing asked helped looked impressed watched wanted	other mother find kind **C2** Bossy E whole used these like made	sister decide explain also fossils pictures extinct family

4. TRICKY WORDS Have students read each row for accuracy, then fluency.

A	does	don't	imagine	front	dinosaurs	5
B	bear	of	lived	been	Earth	10

5. MULTISYLLABIC WORDS Have students read the word by parts, tell how many syllables are in the word, then read the whole word.

A	li•on	lion	rhi•no	rhino
B	dif•fer•ent	different	kan•ga•roo	kangaroo
C	sci•en•tists	scientists	Ne•bras•ka	Nebraska

6. DICTATION Say the word. Have students say the word, then finger count and say the sounds. Have students say each sound as they touch or write it.

A1 Shifty Words	B1 Rhyming Words
s k y s c a r s t ar	th i n k d r i n k b l i n k

70

CAUTION

Your children may not need Extra Practice. Use assessment results to determine if Extra Practice is needed.

5. Multisyllabic Words

For each word, have students read each syllable out loud, finger count the syllables, then tell how many syllables are in the word. If needed, use the word in a sentence. Have students read the whole word.

6. Dictation

sky, scar, star, think, drink, blink

- Say "sky." Have students say the word. Guide students as they finger count and say the sounds. Have students touch or write the sounds, then read the word.

  The first word is **sky.** Say the word. (sky) Say and count the sounds in **sky** with me.

  Hold up one finger for each sound. /s/•/k/•/īīī/ How many sounds? (three)

  What's the first sound? (/sss/) Touch under /sss/.
  What's the next sound? (/k/) Touch under /k/.
  What's the last sound? (/īīī/) Write /īīī/ with the letter . . . y. Read the word. (sky)

- Repeat with "scar" and "star."
- Continue with the rhyming words: think, drink, blink.

PROCEDURES

1. **First Reading**
   Mix group and individual turns, independent of your voice.

2. **Second Reading, Short Passage Practice: Developing Prosody**
   - Demonstrate how to read a line or two with expression.
   - Guide practice with your voice.
   - Provide individual turns while others track with their fingers and whisper read. Provide descriptive and positive feedback.

3. **Partner Reading: Repeated Reading (Checkout Opportunity)**
   While students do Partner Reading, listen to individuals read the passage. Work on accuracy and fluency, as needed.

4. **Homework: Repeated Reading**

EXTRA PRACTICE 3

Unit 10 Fluency Passage

Name ____________

Fluency Passage

My goal is to read with 0–2 errors and ___ words correct per minute.

I read with ___ errors and ___ words correct per minute.

Amazing Fossils

Imagine an animal that had claws like a bird but looked like a bear, a	15
horse, and a rhino.	19
If you think this is a made-up animal, you are wrong. There used	33
to be many different kinds of animals on Earth. These animals are now	46
extinct, but the fossils that we find tell us what they looked like.	59
In Nebraska, scientists did find a fossil of an animal that had claws	72
like a bird but looked like a bear, a horse, and a rhino.	85
Scientists also found a fossil of an animal that was big like a lion but	100
had a pouch like a kangaroo.	106
Thousands of other kinds of fossils have been found. These fossils	117
tell us that the animals that lived long ago were different and amazing.	130

Homework
I've listened to my child read this p... Signed ____________

71

PROCEDURES • ACTIVITY AND WORD FLUENCY A OR B

For each step, demonstrate and guide practice, as needed. Then have students complete the page independently.

1. **Activity**
   Passage Comprehension
   - Have students read each sentence or question, then fill in the bubble and/or blank with the correct answer.
   - Think aloud with students and discuss the multiple-choice options, as needed.

   Paragraph Comprehension
   - Have students read the paragraph.
   - Have students read each numbered sentence, then fill in the bubble and/or blank.
   - Have students read the completed sentences.

   Self-monitoring
   Have students read and check their work.

EXTRA PRACTICE 3

Unit 10 Activity

Name ____________

Passage Comprehension

Amazing Fossils

1. There used to be many different kinds of animals on Earth that are now extinct. How do we know what they looked like?
   - ○ We know what they looked like because they are extinct.
   - ○ Scientists have told stories about dinosaurs for thousands of years.
   - ● The fossils that we find tell us what they looked like.
2. Scientists found a fossil that had claws like a bird. What did they say the animal looked like?
   They say the animal looked like a bear, a horse, and a rhino.
3. Imagine a different and amazing dinosaur. What does it look like?
   It is tall like a giraffe, it has spots, and it has a beak like a bird.

Paragraph Comprehension

Scientists found camel fossils in Nebraska. The fossils tell us camels were different long ago. These camels were taller and had longer necks.

1. How do scientists know that camels lived in Nebraska?
   They found camel fossils in Nebraska.
2. These camels were . . . taller and had longer necks.
   - ○ taller and had short necks.
   - ● taller and had longer necks.

✓ Check and Correct

72

2. **Word Fluency (BLMs are located on the CD.)**
   You may wish to have students repeat practice with Word Fluency A or B.